CREATING YOUR
High School
Resume

A Step-by-Step Guide to Preparing an Effective Resume for Jobs, College, and Training Programs

SECOND EDITION

- Create a resume that highlights your skills, background, and personal qualities
- Learn to describe what you have done and what you can do
- Discover what to include in your resume and how to make it stand out
- Practice writing every part of your resume

Kathryn Kraemer Troutman

Creating Your High School Resume, *Second Edition*

A Step-by-Step Guide to Preparing an Effective Resume for Jobs, College, and Training Programs

© 2003 by Kathryn Kraemer Troutman

Published by JIST Works, an imprint of JIST Publishing, Inc.
8902 Otis Avenue
Indianapolis, IN 46216-1033

Phone: 800-648-JIST   Fax: 800-JIST-FAX
E-mail: info@jist.com   Web site: www.jist.com

Note to instructors. This workbook (*Creating Your High School Resume*) is part of a curriculum that also includes a portfolio workbook (*Creating Your High School Portfolio*) and an instructor's guide. The instructor's guide covers both workbooks. The workbooks can be used separately or together, depending on your class objectives. All materials are available separately from JIST.

Videos on resume writing, portfolio development, and job search topics are also available from JIST. A CD-ROM and Web site with information on over 14,000 jobs is available through CareerOINK.com. The Web site offers information at free and subscription levels. Call 1-800-648-JIST for details.

Quantity discounts are available for JIST products. Have future editions of JIST books automatically delivered to you on publication through our convenient standing order program. Please call 1-800-648-JIST or visit www.jist.com for a free catalog and more information.

Visit www.jist.com. Find out about our products, order a catalog, and link to other career-related sites. You can also learn more about JIST authors and JIST training available to professionals.

Acquisitions Editor: Susan Pines
Development Editor: Veda Dickerson
Cover and Interior Designer: Aleata Howard
Page Layout Coordinator: Carolyn J. Newland
Proofreaders: Stephanie Koutek, Jeanne Clark
Indexer: Jeanne Clark

Printed in the United States of America
09 08 07 06   9 8 7 6 5 4 3

We have been careful to provide accurate information throughout this book, but it is possible that errors and omissions have been introduced. Please consider this in making any career plans or other important decisions. Trust your own judgment above all else and in all things.

Trademarks: All brand names and product names used in this book are trade names, service marks, trademarks, or registered trademarks of their respective owners.

ISBN-13: 978-1-56370-902-9
ISBN-10: 1-56370-902-3

About This Book

If you are like most high school students, you probably have not given much thought to preparing a resume. If you've thought about resumes at all, you may think they are just for parents, teachers, and people with careers. But as a high school student, you will probably find that a resume is your ticket to finding a job. You will use your resume when you apply for internships, training programs, or college.

A resume is a summary of your school courses, grades, academic honors, extracurricular activities, sports participation, work experience, volunteer experience, and special skills. It is a tool you can use to make a good first impression on interviewers.

Creating Your High School Resume is a unique workbook that takes you step-by-step through the resume writing process. It describes what should be included in your resume and provides examples and worksheets to reinforce what you've learned. It shows you how to highlight important information and target your resume to a particular career or education opportunity.

Creating Your High School Resume helps you get a clear picture of yourself—what you have experienced, learned, and accomplished. Your finished resume will not only impress interviewers, it will give you the information and self-confidence you need for making career and education decisions.

Table of Contents

Introduction

Do you struggle with your school assignments? Or do you catch on easily? Do you have little or no work experience? Or does your work record include an internship or apprenticeship? Do you seldom get involved in extracurricular activities? Or are you involved in numerous activities? Do you plan to go to work as soon as you graduate? Or do you plan to get more training and education after high school?

No matter who you are or what your abilities and interests are, this updated version of *Creating Your High School Resume* provides you with valuable resources:

- Resume examples based on real students, including ones who are average or struggling
- Numerous examples of students in technical and vocational programs
- Worksheets for creating a resume step-by-step
- Ideas for using the Web and other technology in resume preparation
- A Job Resume Outline to fill in with the information included in your resumes

Congratulations on deciding to complete this workbook. Your preparation greatly increases your chance of finding success in your life and career!

Special Note from the Author

Teachers and students, please feel free to contact me at **www.resume-place.com** for information about high school resume templates you can use in your computer lab. The templates are based on the resumes in this workbook and will help students prepare the best possible resumes for jobs, college, and training programs.

No author publishes a book without a great deal of help from other people. I would like to thank the people who made this second edition of my book possible: **Lauren, Emily, and Chris** (my children); **Joseph Meersman, Becky Stephens, Kathy Avery, Linda Stevens, Paula Blake, and Janet Ruck** (teachers who offered feedback and allowed me to test the book in high school classes); **professional resume writers** who contributed sample resumes (their names and contact information are noted next to their resume submissions in Chapter 7); **Kalvis and Ligita Kraemer** (high school students who submitted their resumes); **Bonny Kraemer Day** (my sister and editor); and **the production and editorial teams at JIST Publishing.**

Knowing What a Resume Is and Why You Need One

What Are Students Saying?

When I wrote my resume, I learned I have a lot of skills and I can achieve more than I think.

This chapter tells you what a resume is and gives you the reasons why you need a good resume. Your resume can make you more confident of your skills, abilities, and experience. It can help you impress managers and educators who interview you.

If you don't have a resume, you won't have a neat, organized way to let people know about your education, experience, and skills. A good resume makes it easy for you to share this information whenever you need to. Let's get going with your resume now!

Definitions of a Resume

Here are two definitions of a resume:

Dictionary definition of a resume: A summary. A short account of a person's career and qualifications. Usually prepared by a person who is applying for a job.

Author's definition of a high school student's resume: One 8½ × 11 sheet of paper that gives a summary of your high school courses, grades, academic honors, extracurricular activities, sports participation, work experience, volunteer experience, and special skills.

Why a Resume Is So Important

The resume you write in high school is important because it is probably your first resume.

A resume helps you

- Keep track of your education and work experience
- Recognize your skills, interests, and accomplishments
- Save time by attaching your resume to application forms instead of filling out the forms completely
- Make informed college and career choices
- Feel good about yourself and what you have done

As you create your resume, you will be amazed at what you have accomplished. You will see what your interests are—for example, athletics, writing, theater, mechanics, retail, science, technology, sales, politics, journalism, beauty, hospitality, or healthcare. Your high school resume will help you make choices about your future education, technical training, and careers.

> **Tip**
> You may want to update your resume as often as every six months throughout high school. You can easily revise your resume as you add jobs, skills, courses, honors, internships, and activities.

Discovering what you want to do for a career is a major challenge. Your first resume can open doors to career, job, and training opportunities. The resume is your first and best tool for introducing yourself and presenting your skills, education, and experience.

When you begin college, career training, or your first job, you will use your resume often. Your resume will give you confidence and show what you have achieved.

Your Resume Will Grow and Change

Most people change their careers and jobs many times during their lives, especially when they are just getting started. If you change your mind about your interest in a certain type of work, you can change your resume.

For example, right now you may want to be an automotive or aircraft mechanic, so you may be taking technical courses in this area. Later, you may decide to pursue a career as a construction manager. If so, you will have to take new courses, but you will have already learned certain skills while you were studying to become a mechanic. You should emphasize those skills on your resume and show how they can be used in your new career area. In your mechanic's training, you would learn how to read blueprints and manuals and how to work with other people, and those are skills you could also use as a construction manager.

Your activities in high school are important in preparing your first resume because they show you what your interests and abilities are. These activities may give you an advantage when you apply for jobs. They also help you decide what careers you are interested in. For example:

- If you are a high school athlete, you may become a sportscaster, physical education teacher, physical therapist, FBI or CIA agent, police officer, or sales professional. People in these jobs must be disciplined, team players, self-starters, and physically fit!

- If you are active in band and orchestra, you may become a professional musician, composer, music educator, or music therapist. Or you may choose a career that is not connected to music and keep music as a secondary interest.

- If you are interested in theater, debate, or school leadership positions, you may be successful as a lawyer or in a teaching, business, or political career. You probably already have skills in speaking, leadership, research, and management.

Working for the CIA

Do you have interests that might help you be a good CIA agent? If you look on the CIA Web site, you'll find this information about what their undercover (clandestine) positions require:

> For the **extraordinary individual** who wants more than just a job, we offer a unique career—a way of life that will challenge the deepest resources of your intelligence, self-reliance, and responsibility. It demands an adventurous spirit, a forceful personality, superior intellectual ability, toughness of mind, and a high degree of personal integrity, courage, and love of country. You will need to deal with fast-moving, ambiguous, and unstructured situations that will test your resourcefulness to the utmost.

http://www.cia.gov/cia/employment/operational.htm

In addition, your interests outside of school, such as caring for children and senior citizens, working on computers, or fixing cars, may lead you to pursue paid or volunteer work. This work experience will strengthen your resume and help you decide if this job is something you would like to do for a career.

 Realizing that a certain job is *not* for you is as helpful as realizing that it *is*.

This book will help you learn to make your resume fit a variety of jobs. You can do this by emphasizing skills and education that support your objective.

Changing Careers

You can expect to change your career or job at least 10 times in your life. Today's careers are affected by changes in technology, the economy, and other factors such as where people live and how many people live in a certain area. You have to be flexible! Search the Internet for the hottest jobs for new careers! One site you might want to check is the one for the Bureau of Labor Statistics:

http://www.bls.gov

Follow a Student's Changing Resume

In this book, you will see various versions of a resume for a high school student named Emily Thompson. As you read Emily's case study, note how her resume grows and changes based on her evolving interests and career goals. Her resume is written in different ways, and you will learn why.

Your interests, experiences, and grades are sure to be different from Emily's. Many other examples appear in this book to help you recognize your skills and make the most of what you've done.

People continue to use resumes all through their lives. How is your high school resume different from one written by a person who is already working? The main difference is the amount of time and information it covers. The format may be quite similar. You've been in high school two to four years, but someone who is older may have been out of high school for many years. Imagine how hard it is to write a two-page resume about 20 years of experience!

So, make the best of what you have. As you achieve new goals, you will start to change the older information. For now, include all of your important experiences.

Ways to Use a Resume

Resumes serve many practical purposes. The rest of this chapter explains the main ways you will use your resume.

Applying for Jobs

A good resume makes looking for work much easier. Many employers will be impressed if you have a resume as a high school student. To apply for a job, you should e-mail, mail, or hand-deliver your resume and cover letter to the employer. Chapter 6 gives tips for writing a cover letter. Chapter 8 provides information about looking for a job.

NASA Student Jobs

NASA provides job opportunities for students. Check its Web site for details.

http://www.nasajobs.nasa.gov/jobs/
student_opportunities/temporary_stay.htm

Online Job Applications and Resumes

You can use several different methods to submit a resume. Many employers now ask that you send your resume by e-mail. You can also apply for jobs online by copying and pasting your resume into an online resume builder that the company supplies. And, of course, you can mail the resume. Use an envelope that's a little larger than your resume so you do not have to fold your resume. If you do mail your resume, the employer may want to scan it into a database.

You should have a resume both on paper and in an electronic format. You'll see samples of both formats in this book.

To find a job, you can write to the human resources director of a potential employer and ask if the company is hiring summer or part-time high school students. It can't hurt to ask. You may even find a job that is not advertised, and you may find that the employer has a need you can fill.

Also, you may hear about an opening from someone you know, or you might speak to the employer before sending your resume. If so, mention these contacts in your cover letter. Doing so will give you an edge over other people who apply.

You can also find jobs by contacting an employer without having an appointment. Doing this is called cold calling. If you walk in the door of a potential employer and ask for work, you most likely will not get an interview. But you can still introduce yourself to the employee you first see when you come in. Give the person a copy of your resume and explain that you are looking for part-time work. Ask the person to please relay your message and give your resume to the manager.

 Even if a company uses job applications, attach your resume to the application. This will save you time and will impress the person who reviews the application. Keep your jobs, courses, and references up-to-date. Some employers require the job application, but it is okay to attach a resume.

You can also use the Internet, yellow pages, newspapers, and local business research to find jobs. You may respond to classified ads online or by mail, or you may contact a business that you know hires students. If you see an interesting ad in a newspaper or online, send your resume in the mail or by e-mail. Also send a cover letter. Let the company or individual know you're interested and available. Methods for sending your resume by e-mail will be discussed later in this book.

 Be ready with a resume all the time. Many people are looking for hard-working students. You may get job information from your parents, friends of your parents, your friends' parents, business owners, and local businesses. A resume is icing on the cake. These people may think you'd be a good worker, but your resume pulls everything together and proves that you are!

For You

JOB ADVERTISEMENTS

Find at least one newspaper advertisement for a student employee and tape it in the box below.

In the space below, write the addresses for two Web sites where student opportunities are listed.

_____

_____

_____ Put a check mark here to show that you researched student jobs on an Internet job site such as Monster.com.

_____ Put a check mark here to show that you saved or book-marked any ads or organizations that look interesting.

Applying for Internships

An internship is a job, sometimes with pay and sometimes without, that helps you learn a specific task and become familiar with a certain industry. The person or group you work for usually trains you and spends extra time with you.

An internship can give you valuable experience now and help you get a job later. An added benefit is that it will help you develop references for your resume. Some fields in which you can find internships are business, health-care, human services, radio and television, advertising, government, public relations, and publishing.

Most internships require that you apply online. You will be asked to post your resume to a database or send the resume by e-mail to an internship coordinator.

Check Out This Web Site!

Are you looking for information about internships for high school students? The following Web site gives information about what's available, how to apply, and many other resources.

http://www.internjobs.com/resumes.html

In your resume for an internship, you should show that you are sincere, dependable, and interested in the organization. You should also describe your qualifications and tell why you are applying. You must show that you are worthy of a company's time and training.

Some employers may not provide detailed application instructions. The AboutJobs.com Network and InternJobs.com suggest that you follow these steps when applying:

- Write a resume and cover letter that describe the internship and why you are interested in it. This information will be helpful to the internship coordinator. You can apply for the internship even if you don't have much experience. After all, that's why you want the internship. Describe your skills, activities, and interests that make you suited for the internship.

- It is usually best to send your cover letter and resume by e-mail unless the employer asks you not to.

  - Don't use HTML or images within the body of your e-mail.

  - You may want to send your resume and cover letter as e-mail attachments. Write a short note in the textbox telling the employer that you have attached two Word files—one for your resume and one for your cover letter.

  - Another option is to copy and paste your letter and resume into the textbox of the e-mail. Copy the cover letter first, and then the resume. E-mail a copy to a friend to see how it looks. Review and fix any formatting that is not correct.

  - After you send the e-mail application, send your resume and cover letter by mail. The Internet is a great job search tool, but people receive hundreds of e-mails. When your e-mail moves up the screen, it may not be visible to the internship recruiter. The employer will appreciate receiving a paper version also. Indicate in your mailed cover letter that you also sent an e-mail application.

- If you choose not to use e-mail to apply for the internship, you can send your cover letter and resume by mail. Use a large envelope.

- Always remember to thank the employer for the opportunity to apply for an internship with his or her organization.

Applying for Summer Programs

You may have to complete an application and personal statement to apply for summer programs. You can also enclose your one-page resume, which serves as a quick review for the admissions committee. Some programs have many applicants. A resume can set you apart from other applicants by showing that you are professional, sincere, and ready to go.

Applying for Work-Study or Co-op Programs

In a work-study or co-op program, you will spend part of your day taking regular courses and part of your day at a job. This experience gives you good exposure to the workplace before graduation. You are sometimes paid for work-study jobs. You will have a better chance of getting into a work-study or co-op program if you have a good resume.

Doing Volunteer and Community Service Work

Most high schools require volunteer and community service work to graduate. You can find out what opportunities are available by talking with your school guidance counselor and service-learning coordinator. If you have an area of interest (for example, music, social work, animal care, psychology, or business), apply for positions in that field. Remember that volunteers can be a valuable help to an organization.

A volunteer or community service job can help you get a paid position in the same field. Select volunteer and community service positions carefully and look for work that uses your skills and interests.

Apply with a resume so the manager can see your skills and interests. Remember that the employer is giving you an opportunity to learn and to gain a reference for future positions.

Attending College and Technical Job Fairs

Admissions representatives and recruiters are waiting to meet you at these events. If you do not have a resume with you, you will not be very effective. This is your opportunity to introduce these individuals to your experience and interests.

Your resume will be scanned into a database and kept for future job openings. This resume is critical for college admissions, internships, and positions in corporations.

Applying to Technical Training Programs

Technical training programs consist both of classes and of employment or an internship. These programs teach subjects such as automotive technology, computer graphics and design, accounting, or paralegal work. You may receive a certificate that can help you get a job in a specific technical field.

Filling out applications for technical training programs takes time. You can use your resume to answer many questions and then attach a copy of your resume. Be sure your resume lists your related technical skills, like the samples shown in this book do.

Applying to Colleges

An up-to-date resume can help you with your applications and your personal statement. When you have a record of your activities, honors, and courses, you can fill out the applications much faster. Include the resume with your package. It will help admissions representatives understand your background, and you will impress them with your organizational skills.

Your resume can even help you write a college admissions essay. You can look at your resume and write about a significant educational experience that would be of interest to the college admissions representative.

Applying for Scholarships

Many scholarship applications request work samples, personal statements, letters, and other information. You can also enclose your resume to give the scholarship committee a total picture of your education and experience. You will save them time, create a good impression, and help them make a decision about the scholarship.

Finding Mentors

A mentor is a professional person who is successful and experienced in a specific field. A mentor is someone who has time to talk to you occasionally about what it's like to work in a particular occupation. This person will give you ideas about training courses and specialized skills you will need. If your mentor thinks you have the interest, basic skills, and potential to intern or work in a particular field, he or she might refer you to hiring managers of companies in that field.

The following table gives examples of career fields and mentors.

Career Field	Mentor	Suggestions
Computers	Information technology professional	This field offers many kinds of jobs. You should find someone who has the kind of computer job you are seeking (for example: networking, software, systems, Web design, database, or programming).
Engineering	Engineer	Look for someone in the specific engineering field you are seeking (for example: civil, electrical, mechanical, or aerospace).
Fashion or retailing	Store manager or buyer	If you want to work for a major chain, contact someone who is already working in that size company. This is much different than working in a small boutique or small chain.
Sports management	Arena or team manager	Stay involved in sports. You will need a mentor and inside information to get into this field of work.
Writing	Journalist	Find a mentor who does the type of writing you want to do (for example: journalism, online writing, political, research, or government).
Web site development	Webmaster	Start developing Web sites and reading books and articles on Web development and Web design.
Space science	NASA employee or other defense scientist	Look for someone who works for the Air Force or other government agency. Attend workshops and conferences; read NASA and Department of Defense Web sites and articles.

(continues)

(continued)

Career Field	Mentor	Suggestions
Veterinary medicine	Veterinarian or veterinary technician	When you take your pets to the vet, talk to the doctor and the staff. Volunteer or work part-time in a veterinarian's office. Read about this industry online. Go to the Web site for the National Institutes of Health (www.nih.gov) and read about veterinary medicine.
Sales and marketing	Sales manager, sales executive, or advertising executive	Contact a go-getter sales executive. Ask them how they sell and what they love about business and sales. Catch their passion and interest for their work. This work is part personality and part knowledge.
Small business	Storeowner or small business owner	If your family owns a business, you probably already know someone who could be your mentor. If not, get to know business owners or entrepreneurs. Volunteer to work with them (they will be thrilled). Ask questions and listen to the answers. Business owners can make many referrals and give you many ideas. They are usually very willing to help others who want to start businesses.

The way to find a mentor is to read local newspapers to see who has received achievement awards in their field. You can also look online for companies in a particular field. Write to company presidents and ask questions. Volunteer to work. Read and learn. Eventually, ask someone to be your mentor and to provide some insight into his or her field of work. Send the person a resume. (Wait until later to ask for job ideas and referrals.)

How Can You Find a Mentor?

Go to www.google.com. Type in TOP PROFESSIONALS. You will see a list of Web sites that feature outstanding professionals. Look at the sites and read about the people.

I found a site that listed the top professionals in Sarasota, Florida. It included their photos and a description of their work. It did not list their e-mail addresses. If you wanted to contact one of the professionals, you could look in the telephone book or call directory assistance. Then you could call the person's office and ask for the mailing address.

If you write to a professional, you might use this approach: "Congratulations on your achievement. I found your name and description on http://sarasotaworld.com/whoiswho/d.html, Who's Who in Sarasota. I am a junior at Atholton Senior High School in Columbia, MD. May I write to you again and ask questions about your job? Thank you for your time. I look forward to your answer.

Sincerely,

Megan Moran"

For You

A MENTOR

Do some research and find someone who would be a great mentor for you. Fill in the following information about the person.

Person's name: _____

Job title: _____

Company name: _____

Telephone number: _____

Address: _____

List the resources you used to locate this person.

_____

_____

_____

List two things you would like to learn from this person.

1. _____

2. _____

Getting References

A reference is someone who has known you for some time and will recommend you to an employer. Teachers, coaches, school counselors, community leaders, family friends, and ministers make good references. Do not use people in your family as references. After you have some work experience, former supervisors are usually the best references. Decide who you will ask to serve as references. Then, contact those people. You should have two or three references.

After an employer interviews you, he or she may call a reference and ask questions. Some questions might be

- How long have you known this student?

- How do you know this student?

- If the student worked for or with you, what type of work did the student do?

- What are the student's strongest and weakest skills?

- Could you count on the student to be on time?

- If the student worked for you in the past, would you hire the student again?

As you can see from the questions, references are very important. If your references really like you, they will be enthusiastic about your skills and background. This will increase your chances of being hired or accepted into programs. Tell your references what kind of work you're looking for and what you want them to do. This way they won't be surprised when they receive a call from a prospective employer.

Letters of Recommendation

You can also ask your references for letters of recommendation. These letters can be extremely helpful, especially if you are applying for educational or internship programs.

You can give your reference list to your potential employer three ways:

- Send it when you send your resume, but only if requested

- Bring it with you to the interview

- Send it after an interview when the employer is seriously considering you for hire

Your references will be more familiar with everything you have done if they have had a chance to look at your resume. Then, when they receive a call from an interested organization, they will be able to describe your strengths.

Without your resume, they may not know all your activities or honors. Your references will appreciate being able to give complete, knowledgeable information to your potential employers.

Tip Be sure to ask people for permission to use them as references *before* you give their names to potential employers or colleges. Tell your references about your plans so they can keep up with you and your career.

Once you get a job, send a thank-you note and periodic updates to your references. They'll appreciate it and may recommend or refer you to others as you advance in your career.

For You

REFERENCES

List the names of three people who would make good references for you. Describe each person's relationship to you (for example: teacher, pastor, or former employer).

Name: _____

   Relationship to you: _____

Name: _____

   Relationship to you: _____

Name: _____

   Relationship to you: _____

Networking

Networking means introducing yourself and your goals to as many people as possible. It is one of the most successful job search methods you can use.

The people in your network might include your neighbors, former teachers, coaches, relatives, and friends of your parents. One of these people may know of a job, internship, or educational program that would be perfect for you. If you tell people about your interests, they will keep you in mind.

You might think people you know are aware of all you have done in high school. In reality, they may know that you are into sports or that you are good at science, but they won't know everything you have done in and outside of school.

The best way to network is to keep in touch with people and give them copies of your up-to-date resume. You cannot be bashful when you're trying to develop a career and want to succeed.

What's the Difference Between a Mentor and a Network?

Your mentor is your continuing career and educational advisor. This person can give you information about a certain career and recommend courses and internships that will help you.

Your network is a group of people you can contact for job leads or referrals.

Conducting Informational Interviews

Informational interviewing is a common practice among job seekers, college graduates, and people who are interested in a specific career. These interviews give you a chance to ask questions without applying for a job. The goal is to find a person within a certain career field or a certain company in which you might like to work. Ask for an appointment to discuss the individual's job. You can hand or mail the person your resume with a cover letter asking for an informational interview.

Most professionals know what an informational interview is. Don't be bashful about asking for 10 or 15 minutes. If the individual says no, move on to someone who has more time.

Before the interview, research the company. Check its Web site and its mission statements. Read its press releases and employment and services advertisements. Become familiar with all available company information.

During the interview, you can ask questions about what you've read. Write down a few questions, but don't be afraid to ask spontaneous ones. Sometimes these questions will get you the most information. Examples of questions are, "Do you like your job?" and "What do you enjoy most and least about your work?"

How do you find the name of someone to interview? Possible sources are the Internet, newspaper articles, talk shows, and friends. Save the names and numbers of people who might be able to give you information and insight into jobs and careers!

For You

INFORMATIONAL INTERVIEWS

Think of two people who would be great to interview for career information. In the spaces below, fill in the information about each person.

Name: _____

Company name: _____

Job title: _____

Telephone number: _____

E-mail address: _____

Address: _____

_____

Name: _____

Company name: _____

Job title: _____

Telephone number: _____

E-mail address: _____

Address: _____

_____

Joining College or Community Clubs or Associations

Many college and community organizations want to see your background in a resume format before they consider you for enrollment or acceptance. A good resume can make a positive impression and help you land the opportunity to be part of a competitive college organization.

WHAT'S NEXT?

As you learned in this chapter, you can use a resume in many ways—not just in a job search. Start thinking about your resume now. The rest of this book gives you the how-to instructions for looking great on paper.

Chapter 2 will help you understand two types of resumes you might want to use. Your resume will help you feel confident about your achievements, activities, skills, and interests!

Understanding Resume Types

What Are Students Saying?

I have a lot of skills, and I've achieved more than I thought during high school.

This chapter introduces you to the two resume formats used most often by high school students.

The first format described in this chapter is the targeted resume. This is the type of resume that works best for high school students. A targeted resume includes a detailed summary of your skills, using keywords from your selected industry. This skills summary is followed by information about your education and experience. This type of resume presents all relevant information in a way that appeals to the employer or individual you are targeting.

The second format is the chronological resume. This type of resume also provides information about your skills, but your employment and education information is highlighted and is arranged in date order. Start with your high school information and end with your work history and volunteer activities.

Targeted Resumes

A targeted resume highlights the skills and experiences you want to promote to a potential employer or admissions representative. You may not realize it, but you do have skills that can be highlighted! You have developed these special skills in many ways, including the following:

- School courses
- Family experiences
- Work experiences
- Internships
- Volunteer activities
- Extracurricular activities
- Reading
- Interests and hobbies
- Sports
- Travel
- Friendships
- Study habits

A targeted resume includes a detailed summary of your skills. The skills are targeted to a specific position or type of training. Keywords are used to catch the employer's attention and to show that you know the terminology that is used in a particular job. A targeted resume should be no more than one page.

Keywords

Keywords are the terminology used to describe your specific type of work. They are words that a hiring manager or human resources person will identify quickly. These words will show that you know the current language of your industry.

Keywords reflect the skills needed for a job. For instance, if you're applying for an office clerk position, the critical keywords would be *computer skills, verbal skills, customer service, report writing, proofreading, editing, teamwork,* and *organization.*

This type of resume works well for people who are applying for jobs or for career training and in-service programs. Competitive career training programs may require that you show past experience and skills in order to be considered for the program.

Let's summarize. Keep these pointers in mind! A targeted resume:

- ✐ Uses keywords relevant to the targeted position
- ✐ Includes only those experiences which are relevant to the position
- ✐ Should be only one page
- ✐ Works well for people who are applying for jobs or for career training and in-service programs

 As you gain more skills, you may need to delete older and less relevant material. For example, if you're applying for a mechanic's position, you may not need to list the position you held bussing food at a local restaurant.

Chronological Resumes

A chronological resume is a comprehensive resume not targeted in a specific direction, as it would be if you were pursuing a particular career. It is a complete presentation of your qualifications. It lists many items, including the following:

- ✐ Important academic courses and workshops
- ✐ Good grades
- ✐ Sports and other activities
- ✐ Honors and awards
- ✐ Work-study programs and internships
- ✐ Service learning
- ✐ Employment

This type of resume may also include a short section that summarizes your skills. You should list your most significant and special skills. This skills section can help you stand out. Your skills are different from those of other applicants, and the recruiter might be looking for someone just like you! Most recruiters love having this information.

Example of a Skills Summary Section of a Resume

Skills Summary

- ✏ Work well with others

- ✏ Have good communications skills

- ✏ Empathize with other people's needs and concerns

- ✏ Utilize Windows 98, 2000, Microsoft Word, and Access

- ✏ Musician—piano, guitar, and violin

- ✏ Artist—painting, photography, drawing, and sketching

- ✏ Writer—poetry, stories, novels, journal

This type of resume works well for people who are applying for college admission. You also can use a chronological resume to apply for scholarships, to find a mentor, or to distribute at college and job fairs. Your chronological resume, application, personal statement, and resume will be your introduction to the people who make the decisions.

If you want to attend a particular college or training program, make your application package stand out–everything is competitive these days. If you have a major or career interest in mind, make sure your resume includes all your experience, honors, and activities in that area.

Let's summarize. Keep these pointers in mind! A chronological resume

- ✐ Presents a broad, complete profile or review of your education, experience, activities, honors, and other background information

- ✐ Is not targeted toward any particular job or career field

- ✐ Includes a short summary of your skills

- ✐ Can be used to apply for college or training programs, to apply for scholarships, to find a mentor, or to distribute at college and job fairs

Emily's Resumes

Emily's targeted resume. For the summer after graduation, Emily used the targeted resume on page 23 to apply for an internship at Kings Canyon, California. She wanted a position as a trail worker in the Volunteer-in-Parks Program, where she could gain environmental experience that involved hard labor.

This resume did not require specific information on honors, activities, workshops, and publications. Emily needed to show that she could backpack, cut through rocks to make switchbacks, and live in a tent for two months.

Her interests in the environment have evolved. She hopes for a self-designed major in environmental science and creative writing. Notice that the resume on page 23 uses keywords such as horsepacking, minimum impact camping, safety, and field hockey. These keywords reflect the skills needed for the trail worker internship that Emily wanted.

Emily used a targeted resume to apply for a summer internship as a trail worker.

Emily's chronological resume. Emily used the chronological resume on page 24, along with her application and personal statement, to apply to colleges. In this resume, she moved the Education section to the top of the page. She emphasized her writing, teaching, and theater background because she planned to start her college career with a major in creative writing. Notice that she did not use the keywords she used in her targeted resume.

EMILY THOMPSON
43 Village Court
Westboro, MD 00000
Home: (000) 555-5555
E-mail: thompson@ari.net

OBJECTIVE: Trail Worker, Volunteer-in-Parks, Kings Canyon, California

SUMMARY OF RELEVANT SKILLS AND EXPERIENCE

Outdoor Leadership Experience
National Outdoor Leadership School, Lander, WY, Summer XXXX
Graduated Rocky Mountain Horsepacking course involving one week of ranch experience and two weeks of backcountry travel in the Wind River range. Trained in minimum impact camping, backpacking, and horsepacking. Emphasis on backcountry leadership skills necessary to lead future personal expeditions: safety and judgment, leadership and teamwork, outdoor skills, environmental ethics, and horse handling and packing skills.

Interpretation Skills
Internship, Haleakala National Park, Maui, HI, Fall XXXX
Interpretation at high-volume visitor center and development of special projects, including park displays and 20-minute naturalist visitor programs. Hiked inside the volcano six miles.
High School Public Speaking
Experienced researcher and writer in high school and community publications. Four years' experience in theater and debate competitions.

Sports and Athletic Experience
Member, varsity field hockey team, XXXX
Enjoy hiking, backpacking, and camping
Physically fit

EDUCATION
Westboro High School, Westboro, MD. Expect to graduate May XXXX.
Honor Roll, average GPA 3.8/4.0, XXXX–present

EXPERIENCE
File Clerk and Runner, Trafalgar & Associates, Ft. Collins, CO, Summer XXXX

EMILY THOMPSON
43 Village Court, Westboro, MD 00000
Home: (000) 555-5555
E-mail: thompson@ari.net

EDUCATION

Westboro High School, Westboro, MD. Expect to graduate May XXXX.

Academic Honors:

Honor Roll, average GPA 3.8/4.0, XXXX–present

Advanced Placement: U.S. History and English coursework

Activities:

Editor-in-Chief, *Phoenix Literary Arts Magazine,* XXXX–XXXX

Maryland State Forensics League, President
    Debate National Competitor: Kansas City, KS (XXXX); Milwaukee, WI (XXXX); Detroit, MI (XXXX)

Dramatic Theater: *Twelve Angry Jurors; Flowers for Algernon*; leading role in *You Can't Take It with You*

WORKSHOPS

Hawaiian Language and Culture, Maui Community College, Maui, HI, Fall XXXX

Writing and Thinking, Lewis College, Seattle, WA, Summer XXXX

National Outdoor Leadership School, Lander, WY, Summer XXXX

Andre Braugher (*Homicide* series) Shakespeare Workshop, Winter XXXX

Writer's Workshop, State University, Frederick, MD, Summer XXXX

HONORS AND RECOGNITION

Winner of Redmond College's "Women Writing about Women" Competition, April XXXX, one of three selected out of 140 portfolios entered

PUBLISHED POETRY

Salt of the Earth literary magazine

Singing Sands Review

The Apprentice Writer

Featured reader in publicized Fells Point and Baltimore poetry readings

EXPERIENCE

Internship, Haleakala National Park, Maui, HI   Sept.–Dec. XXXX
    Interpretation and special projects.

Teacher's Aide, Newton Elementary School, Baltimore, MD   Spring XXXX

COMPUTER SKILLS

PC and Macintosh Systems: Windows 2000, Microsoft Office Suite, Word 8.0, WordPerfect 8.0

Targeted Resume Examples

On pages 27–29 are three examples of targeted resumes prepared by high school students. Here is some information that will help you understand each student's unique situation.

Searching for Keywords for Your Resume

Brian searched the Internet for some good keywords for his resume. He found an article about Web jobs that referred to a job called "User Tester." A person doing this job would present new computer products to people who might use the products.

Here are some of the words Brian found in the article. He will want to use some or all of these when preparing his resume for a summer internship in Web design and management.

Words showing personal skills needed:

- communicates with a wide variety of people
- communicates with people being tested
- understands what people say
- analyzes and interprets results accurately
- communicates results to coworkers
- notes research trends
- tracks common elements of what is and is not said

Words showing computer-related competencies:

- codes HTML
- recognizes browser- and platform-specific HTML quirks
- understands conditional HTML
- understands basic UNIX
- troubleshoots file permissions and backend problems
- sees instantly how a Web page or site was put together or assembled
- understands the functions a given line of code performs
- has basic understanding of JavaScript and CGI-bin scripting

Future Web Developer

Brian Smith's targeted resume is on page 27. While a junior, Brian used this resume to apply for a summer internship using his Web site design and management skills. At www.webmonkey.com, he found articles for college students and interns that helped him determine what terms to use in describing his skills.

Future Small-Engine Mechanic

John McIntyre's resume is on page 28. John recognizes his interest, experience, and skills in working with engines. He has been doing mechanical work since he was 15. He wants to get additional career training after high school and become certified so he can own his own business or work as a mechanic. He used the following targeted resume to apply for a career training program.

John's Questions and Answers

What did you like best about writing your resume?
It showed me that I can do things and describe them to other people.

What did you like least?
It took too long.

Future Police Officer

Clifford Kraft's resume is on page 29. Clifford was inspired to become a police officer because he saved his stepmother's life. He is a Commander in ROTC, a peer assistant, and a boy scout, and he has CPR certification and wrestling experience. He used the following targeted resume to apply for acceptance into the police academy.

Clifford's Questions and Answers

What did you like best about writing your resume?
It helped me find out what I am good at.

What did you like least?
All the writing we had to do.

Brian Smith
6609 Kilimanjaro Road
Columbia, MD 21045
(410) 777-7777
Briansmith777@yahoo.com

OBJECTIVE:
Seeking an internship in Web development.

SKILLS SUMMARY:
COMMUNICATIONS SKILLS:
Ability to communicate with and understand exactly what people are saying. Patient and understanding with non-technical users. Able to communicate during design, testing, and problem-solving.
ANALYTICAL SKILLS:
Analytical skills to analyze technical information, content, and user needs. Detail-oriented in managing information and results for important Web site improvements. Able to explain information effectively.
TECHNICAL SKILLS:
Able to code in HTML; familiar with browser- and platform-specific HTML quirks, as well as server-side problems. Able to troubleshoot file permissions and backend problems. Able to put together pages, as well as understand code platforms. Knowledge of JavaScript and CGI-bin scripting.

EDUCATION:
Oakland Mills High School, Columbia, MD
Expect to graduate May XXXX

Activities:　JV Baseball–XXXX
　　　　　　Varsity Baseball–XXXX

Honors:　Student of the Quarter for Science in XXXX
　　　　　Student of the Month; English and CRD I
　　　　　Honor Roll multiple times

Courses:　Software Apps I, Spanish I and II, Sociology I,
　　　　　Weights I and II, Art I

WORK HISTORY:
Web Designer/Maintainer/Web Master
MDUSAG, Columbia, MD　　　　　March XXXX to June XXXX

Designed, implemented, and maintained Web pages and associated graphics; posted rules and regulations; posted schedules and scores; and published monthly newsletter as appropriate for clients.

COMMUNITY SERVICE:
Owen Brown Middle School, Columbia, MD

Environmental cleanup, tree planting, and grounds improvement, XXXX–XXXX (75 hours)

EXTRACURRICULAR ACTIVITIES:
Play baseball, football, basketball, and racquetball; lift weights; swim; and run.

REFERENCES:
Available upon request.

JOHN A. MCINTYRE

9120 St. John's Lane, Ellicott City, MD 21045 (410) 777-7777
JMcIntyre@earthlink.net

OBJECTIVE:

To obtain a position as a small- or large-engine specialist.

SKILLS SUMMARY:

- Solid problem solving and problem identification skills
- Able to follow directions and pay attention to details
- Excellent engine analyzing skills
- Training and experience in small- and large-engine repair and maintenance
- Ability to meet deadlines and complete tasks
- Hard worker with positive attitude

EDUCATION:

ST. JOHN'S HIGH SCHOOL, Ellicott City, MD
Expect to graduate in May 2003
Activities: Wrestling - 2 years

WORK HISTORY:

J & I Enterprises, Columbia, MD   XXXX–XXXX
MECHANIC
Repair and test various types of lawn equipment, lawn mowers, weed trimmers for commercial and
residential customers.

Jiffy Lube, Columbia, MD   XXXX–XXXX
GENERAL EMPLOYEE/MECHANIC TRAINEE
Changed oil and checked all fluids on automobiles and trucks for customers. Trained in basic engine
maintenance and repair.

Williamson Construction, Baltimore, MD   XXXX–XXXX
SMALL-ENGINE MECHANIC
Repaired and serviced all small-engine equipment.

REFERENCES:

Work and personal references can be supplied on request.

Clifford Kraft

5906 Bonneview Drive
Columbia, MD 20043
cliffordkraft@aol.com

OBJECTIVE: To become a police officer

SUMMARY OF SKILLS

Have lifeguard certification
Work well with others, friendly
Value punctuality and task completion
Have CPR certification

EDUCATION

Oakland Mills High School, Columbia, Maryland

Graduating: Expect to graduate in May XXXX

Activities: ROTC
Wrestling

Honors: Honor student
Saved my stepmother's life
Honor Roll athlete

Courses: CRD, ROTC, Peer Assistant

WORK HISTORY

Lifeguard

Columbia Association, Columbia, MD, May XXXX–Present
Maintain the pool facility, check the chlorine in the pool, enforce pool
rules to ensure safety of all swimmers, provide assistance as needed

COMMUNITY SERVICE
Oakland Mills High School, Columbia, MD
Help the students do real-life jobs (Peer Assistant)

EXTRACURRICULAR ACTIVITIES: Boy Scouts, Swimming, Karate

RECOMMENDATIONS: Available on request

Chronological Resume Examples

On pages 31 and 32 are two examples of chronological resumes prepared by high school students. Here is some information that will help you understand each student's unique situation.

Future Teacher

Alison Rogers' resume is on page 31. Alison has been working with kids throughout middle school and high school. She likes children, is patient, and wants to become a teacher. She used the following chronological resume to apply for college.

Alison's Questions and Answers

What did you like best about the resume writing process?

Getting to type it on the computer and put it into the resume format.

What did you like least?

Having to go back and change every little detail after I fixed it and thought it was fine.

Future Information Technology Professional

Brian Smith's chronological resume is on page 32. You've already looked at his targeted resume (page 27). Brian has been in Web development and design for three years—since middle school. He's obviously going to stay in this field. He will attend either college or career training courses that will give him the best background for Web design, development, and technology related to Internet services. He used this chronological resume to apply for a career-training program.

Brian's Questions and Answers

What are your feelings about the resume writing process?

I believe the process made it easier to explain all the steps in writing a resume.

What did you like least about the resume writing process?

Knowing all the errors I've made.

Alison Sarah Rogers

7777 Rogers Lane, Columbia, MD 21045, (410) 444-3333
E-mail: alisons111@net.com

Objective:

To receive a college degree that will qualify me for an elementary school teaching position.

Skills Summary:

- Patient and understanding with children
- Honest and hardworking
- Work well with other coworkers
- Communicate well orally and in writing
- Utilize PCs with PowerPoint, WordPerfect, Excel, and Access
- Enthusiastic and willing to learn

Education:

OAKLAND MILLS HIGH SCHOOL, Columbia, MD
Expect to graduate in May of XXXX

Activities:	Three years in Future Educators of America (FEA)
	Class of XXXX Fundraising (car washes)
Honors:	Bronze Honor Roll, XXXX–XXXX
	Student of the Quarter/Month-CRD 1
Courses:	Software Applications I & II, Spanish I & II

Employment:

TEACHER'S ASSISTANT

Columbia's Youth Care, Columbia, MD (12 hours/week), January XXXX to present
Patiently play creative games with children, responsibly watch children, and prepare activities and snacks.

CASHIER/COOK

Jerry's Subs and Pizza, Columbia, MD (18 hours/week), Sept. XXXX–June XXXX
Provided food under a tight schedule, took food orders, and ran cash register. Maintained sanitation standards.

BABYSITTER

Williams Family, Columbia, MD (15 hours/week), Summer XXXX
Supervised two children, ages 1 and 3. Planned activities and prepared lunch, dinner, and snacks. Ensured safety.

Community Service:

Howard County Food Bank, Columbia, MD (70 hours), XXXX–XXXX

BRIAN SMITH

6609 Kilimanjaro Road, Columbia, MD 21045
E-mail: Briansmith777@yahoo.com
Phone: (410) 777-7777

OBJECTIVE:

Seeking a career in Information Technology specializing in Web Design and Development.

SKILLS SUMMARY:

- Web skills: HTML and Java knowledge
- Computer skills: Microsoft Word, PowerPoint, FrontPage
- Outgoing and spontaneous
- Good memory and attitude
- Friendly and work well with others
- Patient and understanding

EDUCATION:

OAKLAND MILLS HIGH SCHOOL, Columbia, MD
Expect to graduate May XXXX

Activities:	JV Baseball–XXXX
	Varsity Baseball–XXXX
Honors:	Student of the Quarter for Science in XXXX
	Student of the Month: English and CRD I
	Honor Roll multiple times
Courses:	Software Apps I, Spanish I and II, Sociology I,
	Weights I and II, Art I

WORK HISTORY:

WEB DESIGNER / MAINTAINER / WEBMASTER
MDUSAG (mdusag.com), Columbia, MD   March XXXX to June XXXX
Designed, implemented, and maintained Web pages and associated graphics for professional association of Maryland gymnastics organizations. Posted rules and regulations for the organization, posted state meet schedules and scores, and published monthly client newsletters.

COMMUNITY SERVICE:

Owen Brown Middle School, Columbia, MD. Environmental cleanup, tree planting, and grounds improvement, XXXX–XXXX (75 hours)

EXTRACURRICULAR ACTIVITIES:

Play baseball, football, basketball, and racquetball; lift weights; swim; and run.

For You

THE RIGHT RESUME TYPE

Circle reasons you might need a resume:

To apply for a job

To enroll in a career training program

To apply for college

To apply for scholarships

To find a mentor

To distribute at college and job fairs

For other uses: _____

_____

Which type of resume—targeted or chronological—do you think would work best for you? Why?

_____

_____

_____

_____

WHAT'S NEXT?

You've now completed Chapter 1 and Chapter 2. You know that there are two basic kinds of resumes—targeted and chronological. You've also seen several good high school resumes. In Chapter 3, you will take the next step and begin writing your resume. You'll look at one section of your resume at a time. You may be surprised that you can outline your resume in about one hour!

3

Writing Your Resume

What Are Students Saying?

I liked writing my resume. It shows my skills and abilities, the jobs I've had, and how much school I've completed.

Many students think they don't have anything to include on a resume. Does that describe you? If so, think again. This chapter will guide you through all the sections of your resume, except the skills and objective sections. You will learn to write those sections in Chapters 4 and 8. If you answer all the questions in Chapter 3, your resume will be well under way.

One Section at a Time

The best way to write your resume is one section at a time. By focusing on each section, you will think about every aspect of your education and experience. Then you will list information under each section heading.

By organizing your information into sections, you (and the people reading your resume) will recognize the significance of everything you've done. Don't worry if you have little or nothing to write for certain sections. Include whatever information you can. Then get busy finding activities and courses that appeal to you and are worth adding to your resume. You can

- Join a group or club that interests you
- Take a course or workshop in a specialized field
- Apply for jobs that add quality skills to your resume

- Learn new technical or computer skills
- Apply for an internship
- Do volunteer or community service work that shows you care about people, the environment, or a certain cause

Where to Look for Student Opportunities

You can use the Internet to find student internships, volunteer activities, and cooperative programs for students. Getting involved in one of these activities will provide you with valuable experience you can include on your resume. Consider federal government high school internships and cooperative programs. Look for opportunities at

www.studentinternships.gov

As you complete the activities in this chapter, you will develop your resume section by section. When you are finished, you will have a document that completely represents *you*.

In Chapter 2, you learned about two types of resumes—chronological resumes and targeted resumes. You don't have to decide now which type of resume you will write. Just write down basic information about yourself.

As you begin writing down information to use in your resume, list everything now. Later, look over it again and fine-tune it. As you saw from the sample resumes in Chapter 2, the students selected education, experience, and skills that paint an interesting picture of their high school years. Creating their final resumes was easier after the students made a complete list of everything they had done.

Contact Information

A prospective employer needs to know how to contact you. The employer will want to see your name in large bold type with your address, telephone number, and e-mail address clearly listed. Be creative. Arrange this section any way you choose. See Chapter 5 for other formatting ideas.

Here are some examples of how to arrange this information.

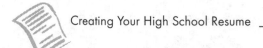

Samantha A. Greene

17 Cherokee Avenue / Catonsville, MD 20233
(555) 555-0000 / E-mail: greene@net.net

KIERA M. KRUEGER
79 Carmel Street
Long Beach, California 95900
(555) 555-9999
kiera777@earthlink.com

CAROLYN ANNE HOBART

One Valley Lane
Utica, New York 76655
Home (555) 555-7777
E-mail: hobart@com.com

CHRIS LANSING

53 Ridge Road, Katy, Texas 99999
Home (555) 555-6666
E-mail: lansing@net.net

MICHAEL G. ANDERS

500 Delaware Street • Pemberton, WA 95544 • (555) 555-4444

RHONDA S. ROBERTS
43 KING BOULEVARD
DETROIT, MI 88888
(555) 555-2222

THOMAS BAKER, III
47 CREEK PLACE
CHEVY CHASE, MD 45554

PHONE/FAX: (555) 555-8888   E-MAIL: TBAKER@NET.NET

STEVEN APPLEGATE

42C W. 90th Avenue   Phone (555) 555-4321
New York, NY 77777   Beeper (555) 555-1234

Nancy E. Day

School address   *Home address*
14 Smythe Street   121 Long Street
Ft. Washington, MD 55555   Westminster, MD 55555
(555) 555-0000—Messages   (555) 555-5555—Home

Tip How you arrange your contact information depends on how crowded your resume is. (Yes, your resume may get crowded!) Note that you can put your address and phone number on one line to save space.

For You

CONTACT INFORMATION

Write your name and contact information here. Arrange them the way you want them to appear on your resume. This will be helpful when you go to your computer to lay out the resume. You may want to try several arrangements, based on the examples.

_____

_____

_____

_____

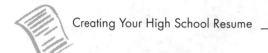

Education

The Education section of your resume should include the name, city, and state of your high school and your expected graduation date. Also list specific academic information, such as college entrance test scores and special courses. Your GPA can be listed if it is over 3.0. Include courses in languages, advanced placement, computers, and electives. Here are examples of ways you can arrange your education information.

Catonsville High School, Catonsville, MD
Graduation expected June XXXX
Gifted and Talented English and Social Studies courses, XXXX–present
Advanced Placement U.S. History, XXXX

THOMAS R. PROCTOR HIGH SCHOOL, Utica, NY
Graduation June XXXX
Overall GPA 3.0/4.0
Computer courses: PCs with Windows, Microsoft Word, and Microsoft Excel

---

CARIZZO SPRINGS HIGH SCHOOL, Carizzo Springs, TX
Expect to graduate May XXXX
Related coursework:

- Agriculture and Livestock Management
- Biology I, II
- Environmental Sciences I
- Spanish I, II, III
- Business Management and PCs

CALIFORNIA HIGH SCHOOL, San Ramon, CA
Graduated May XXXX
Grade Point Average 3.62/4.00
SAT Verbal 560; Math 710
Advanced Placement: AP Calculus
AP English Composition and Literature

For You

EDUCATION

What is the name of your high school? Where is it located (city and state)?

_____

_____

What year do you expect to graduate?_____

What special courses have you taken or are you taking? If your grades are high, list them.

_____

_____

_____

_____

List your SAT and ACT test scores if they would make a good impression.

_____

_____

List your GPA if it is above 3.0.

_____

Honors and Awards

Your honors and awards show that you have skills and are dedicated. If you don't have honors and awards you can list now, think what you might do to earn this kind of recognition. Here are some examples of the Honors and Awards section of high school resumes.

HONORS

National Honor Society	XXXX–present
National Merit Scholar Honorable Mention	XXXX
Second Place in Catonsville High School Math Contest	XXXX

Musical Honors

- Distinguished Maryland Scholar, Talent in the Arts finalist
- Passed Associated Board of the Royal School of Music theory tests with distinction—grades 2 and 3
- Passed Associated Board of the Royal School of Music practical exams with distinction—grades 4 and 5

Athletic Awards

Varsity Basketball, MVP	XXXX
Athlete of the Year, County School System	XXXX
All-Baltimore County, Honorable Mention (basketball)	XXXX

HONORS

Region 81 Champion Team Roper, XXXX
Rodeo State Finalist (Calf Roping and Team Roping), XXXX, XXXX
Lone Star Farmer, XXXX
Member, 4-H Club—raised show lambs

HONORS

- Honored by Bloomsburg Parks & Recreation Association for outstanding service for volunteerism for early childhood after-school program, XXXX–XXXX
- Received third place, Candid Photography Contest, Washington Post, May XXXX
- Received a certificate for participation in children's programs, Bethany Baptist Church, XXXX

For You

HONORS AND AWARDS

List your honors and awards. Include dates. For example, if you were a champion swimmer or received a certificate for participating in an essay contest, write that information here. You never know when you might need the item for a targeted resume. You can organize and edit the Honors and Awards list as needed when you write a resume for a certain purpose.

List honors and awards you received through community events and teams.

_____

_____

List honors and awards you received through your studies.

_____

_____

List honors and awards you received through special academic programs.

_____

_____

List honors and awards you received through contests.

_____

_____

List honors and awards you received through your school extracurricular activities and sports.

_____

_____

Activities

By looking at your Activities section, employers and college admissions staff can learn what you are like and what you can do. If you haven't been involved in student activities, consider joining a club or other group soon. For example, the following Activities sections indicate certain qualities.

Activities:
Four years on wrestling team
Member of JV Wrestling Team—Winters, XXXX–XXXX
Member of Varsity Wrestling Team—Winters, XXXX–XXXX

ACTIVITIES:
Asian Club, SGA, French Club, International Club

Activities:
Dance Company—3 years
Cheerleading—7 years
Art Club—1 year

For You

ACTIVITIES

Record all your high school activities. Include the name of the group or organization, the titles of any positions you held, and the dates when you participated. Make a complete list here that you can edit later. Add to the list as you add new activities.

_____

_____

_____

_____

_____

_____

Workshops and Lessons

If you are lucky enough to have completed summer programs and workshops, they are great for your resume. Specialized training is offered in sports, computers, writing, languages, drafting, music, theater, and many others interest areas. If you haven't participated in workshops or taken lessons, think about taking advantage of opportunities available to you. Ask your teachers, counselors, coaches, and school sponsors about these opportunities.

Here is an example of how this section of your resume might look.

WORKSHOPS and LESSONS

- Workshop on Peer Mediation, James Madison High School, Dallas, TX, XXXX
- Writers' Workshop, Susquehanna University, Roscoe, TX, XXXX
- Peabody Institute, Dallas, TX, Private piano study, XXXX to present
- Outward Bound Program, Toronto, Canada, Spring XXXX
- Kanagawa Lacrosse Exchange to Japan, Summer XXXX

For You

WORKSHOPS AND LESSONS

List workshops and lessons you have attended. Include the sponsoring organization or individual's name and the years you attended.

_____

_____

_____

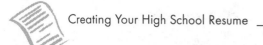

Internships

An internship should be presented just like a job on your resume. Not every student will have intern experience. If you do, that's great! Here's an example:

Geriatric Assistant
Sunrise Assisted Living Corp., Chicago, IL   Summer XXXX
   Assisted 25 residents of assisted living home with daily living needs and activities.

An internship at an advertising agency helps develop skills in proofreading, oral and written communication, and client service.

For You

INTERNSHIPS

   List your internship job title. Tell where you worked and when. Describe your areas of responsibility.

   _____

   _____

   _____

Work-Study or Co-op Programs

A position held through a work-study program should be presented like a job on your resume. Again, not every student will have this kind of experience. If you do, be sure to include it in your resume. Here's an example:

U.S. Army Corps of Engineers, Sugar Land, TX   Spring XXXX
Field Technician. Field sampling and lab testing for government and commercial customers. Hands-on experience in laboratory testing facility. Familiar with OSHA, DNR, and EPA environmental compliance regulations for hazardous materials handling and construction.

For You

WORK-STUDY OR CO-OP PROGRAMS

List the name of the work-study or co-op program in which you participated. Include the name of the organization and the dates you were in the program. List your job title and your areas of responsibility.

_____

_____

_____

Technical Training Programs

On your resume, describe the technical training program in which you participated. Include relevant courses, the company for which you worked, your title, dates, and areas of responsibility. If you were certified through the program (such as in CPR or cosmetology), be sure to list that information. Refer to the following twelve samples.

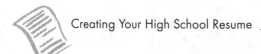

Allied Health Tech Prep Program—Direct Patient Care

Major Courses

Emergency Medical Technology	Kinesiology
Anatomy	Fitness Evaluations
Physiology	Direct Care Services

Meridian Healthcare, Cheyenne Wells, CO, Spring XXXX
Geriatric Technician. Skills developed include patient care, activity planning, family and physician communications.

Certificates
CPR and First Aid, American Red Cross

Culinary Arts and Restaurant Management

Major Courses:

Restaurant Management	Food Preparation and Baking
Purchasing	Computerized Inventory Control
Menu Planning	Sanitation

Olde Philadelphia Inn, Pine Busk, NY   January XXXX–present
Banquet Assistant. Training in food preparation for banquets and full-service meals. Assisted chef with menu planning, buying, and inventory control. Maintained sanitation in kitchen.

Certification: New York State Sanitation Certification

Cosmetology

Major Courses – Completed 1,500 hours theoretical and clinical courses in styling and aesthetician training, including Chemistry, Dermatology, Anatomy, Physiology, and Sanitation.

Related Experience – Stylist and Assistant Aesthetician, Eastern Salon, Los Alamitos, CA, Spring XXXX. Trained and experienced in hair styling, customer service, and sales. Familiar with inventory management, product knowledge, and skin care consultation. Knowledgeable about dermatology, cosmetology, and general shop standards.

License – Passed the State of California Board Examination, April XXXX

Automotive Technology

Major Courses:
Instruction and training in all aspects of automobile operation and service, including Diagnostic Equipment, Computerized Automotive System Simulators, Estimating, and Parts Reference and Selection

Ridgeway Motors, Redondo Beach, CA   *Spring XXXX–present*
Mechanic's Assistant

- Training and experience in diagnosis and repair of automotive systems.
- Skilled in estimating, parts reference, buying, and selection.
- Utilized computerized automotive systems in the shop and classroom.

COMPUTER INFORMATION TECHNOLOGY

Major Courses
Extensive hands-on lab experience with PCs, networks, and databases. Experienced with Novell networks, Access databases, and troubleshooting PCs. Microsoft Office, Windows 2000, and XPSystems training

Computer Technician
Brown & Brown, Colorado Springs, CO   Summer XXXX
- Installed, repaired, and troubleshot PC systems for stand-alone and networked systems.
- Installed and upgraded software programs, including Windows XP.
- Installed Internet browsers, set up ISPs, and assisted users with new systems and e-mail.

Computer Programmer
Bureau of Census, Fruita, CO   Summer XXXX
- Performed programming in C language, primarily to assist with upgrading programs for the year XXXX census.
- Assisted with user questions.

Computer-Aided Drafting and Design

Major Courses

Structural Drafting and Design	Architectural Design
Civil Drafting	Blueprint Reading
Electromechanical Drafting	AutoCAD
Five courses in advanced math and science	

CAD Operator   Summer XXXX–Spring XXXX
Rogers Contractors, Lansing, MI

- Utilized AutoCAD to produce blueprints for civil engineering, including real property, roads, landscaping, irrigation, and buildings.
- Assisted with copying blueprints and organizing customer presentations.

COMPUTER GRAPHICS AND DESIGN

Major Courses

Copy and Art Preparation	Graphic Communication
Advertising and Packaging	Scanning and Photoshop II
Portfolio Development	Adobe Illustrator
PageMaker Digital Copy Preparation	

Computer Graphics Assistant
Stockton Graphics, Wilmington, NC   Summer XXXX–present

- Utilized PC with Microsoft Office, Adobe, and scanning systems.
- Produce graphics for overheads, brochures, letterhead, and Web sites.
- Familiar with HTML programming and integration of .jpg and .psd graphic files.

CONSTRUCTION TECHNOLOGY—PLUMBING AND HVAC

Major Courses

Hand and Power Tools   Electrical Theory   Strength and Materials
Foundation Layout   Blueprint Reading   Job Estimating

Plumber's Assistant – Anderson Plumbing
Schenectady, NY (Fall XXXX–present)

- Install and maintain water supply systems, waste removal systems, fixtures, and gas appliances for residential homes.

HVAC Intern/Project Assistant – Madison Contractors
Saratoga Springs, NY (Summers, XXXX and XXXX)

- Worked on new HVAC plant installation at University of Maryland, Baltimore County campus.
- Assisted with construction, tear-out, and installation of large plant.
- Familiar with safety provisions and digital controls.
- Learned the basics for installation of central air, heat pumps, oil furnaces, and light commercial units.

ELECTRONICS

MAJOR COURSES:

Troubleshooting Techniques   Power Supplies
Electronic Circuits   Testing Equipment and Techniques
Analog and Digital Electronics   Microprocessor Circuits

INTERNSHIP:

West Florida Electric, Sarasota, FL   Spring XXXX–present

- Perform bench work repair and assist with manufacturing plant field visits
- Use knowledge of power supplies, amplifiers, oscillators, and transceivers
- Skilled with test equipment

Legal Assistant/Paralegal Studies

Major Courses:

Legal Research Methods—Lexis/Nexis   Computerized Document Control
Principles of Law   Legal Institutions

Summer Law Clerk/Courier,
Law Offices of Tom Graham, Missoula, MT   Summer XXXX

Utilized PC to help prepare correspondence, pleadings, and memoranda under direct supervision of associate attorney. Scheduled appointments. Became familiar with legal formats, computer systems, court calendar, and case management systems.

ACCOUNTING

Major Courses

Debits and Credits	Economics
Intro to Accounting Software	Accounting I & II

Mark Morrison, CPA, Atlanta, GA

Accounting Assistant. Assisted with compiling tax returns and inputting information for individual clients and small businesses. Utilized QuickBooks and Microsoft Money. Scheduled appointments. (Spring and Summer XXXX)

SECRETARIAL/OFFICE AUTOMATION

Major Courses

Computers: Microsoft Office-Word 97, Excel, PowerPoint
Systems and Administration   Communications Skills

Landmark Insurance, Old Westbury, NY   Spring XXXX–present

Secretary to Insurance Broker. Assist with preparation of correspondence, policies, and presentations. Utilize Microsoft Word, Excel, and Publisher. Manage e-mail and voice mail messages. Input data into Access database.

For You

TECHNICAL TRAINING PROGRAMS

List your technical training position. Include the company name, your job title, dates, and areas of responsibility. If you were in training most of the time, list the types of training you received.

_____

_____

_____

Volunteer and Community Service Work

Volunteer and community service positions are the same as paid positions in terms of your duties within the organization. If you don't have this kind of experience, consider getting involved soon. Community organizations would be thrilled to hear from you.

Be sure to include all your volunteer and community service jobs on your resume. Add the description of your experience to your resume like a paid job. This section of your resume might look like one of the following examples.

TAP'S HORSE FARM, Boulder, CO   Summers XXXX, XXXX
Walker—Assisted with training horses, exercised and groomed animals. Cleaned stalls. Ran errands for staff. Walked horses for developmentally disabled young riders; ensured their safety and enjoyment of the experience.

Volunteer, Taos Emergency Food Ministries, Taos, NM
School Years, XXXX–XXXX
- Assisted with activities of nonprofit service organization, including office duties, inventory, direct mail distribution, and fund-raising.
- Responded to telephone inquiries regarding needs and services.

VOLUNTEER ACTIVITIES
- Steel drum musician performing at schools, retirement centers, and private parties, XXXX–present
- Play piano at El Paso Methodist Church Services, XXXX–present
- Assisted the music program for Vacation Bible School at El Paso United Methodist Church, XXXX–XXXX

Camp Counselor, Spring Blossom Playground, Red Bluff, CA   Summer XXXX
Supervised play and lunch. Accompanied day trips for children aged four to ten.

Hospital Volunteer, Glendale Hospital, Glendale, CA   Summer XXXX
Responsible for transporting wheelchair-bound patients, handling basic medical tasks, answering phones, and filing papers in hospital recovery room.

Volunteer, Pasadena Manor Nursing Home, Pasadena, CA   Summer XXXX
Helped organize and run senior activities.

For You

VOLUNTEER AND COMMUNITY SERVICE WORK

List the names of the companies or organizations where you did volunteer or community service work. For each position, list the dates and your title. Describe your duties.

_____

_____

_____

Work Experience

This section of your resume will show potential employers and college and career training recruiters your

- Skills and industry experience
- Level of responsibility and capability
- Knowledge of customer and product information
- Ability to communicate and work with the public
- Ability to handle multiple tasks
- Interest in helping pay for personal expenses

Here are examples of how to present work experience on your resume:

NOPOLIS FAMILY, Colorado Springs, CO   Summers, XXXX & XXXX
 Nanny. Responsible for the daily activities, safety, and care of two children, ages 8 and 10. Managed a busy schedule consisting of swim team, parties, and day trips in cooperation with parents.

YAGER'S BAGELS, Utica, NY   XXXX-present
 Bagel Prep/Cashier. Under tight production schedules, prepare bagel sandwiches for up to 150 customers per day. Use proper health and safety precautions. Provide customer services and operate cash register.

TEACHER'S AIDE, VAIL MOUNTAIN SCHOOL, Vail, CO   XXXX
- Assisted teachers with after-school activities of 35 second-grade students.
- Planned activities and program materials.
- Provided one-on-one and group instruction and stories.
- Created a mini-theater activity involving student actors using their imaginative ideas for the play.

CROSS-COUNTRY INSURANCE, Springfield, IL   Summer XXXX
Office Assistant. Utilized PC with Windows and Word 2000 to produce correspondence and policyholder reports. Answered telephones, screened calls, and took detailed messages. Researched customer inquiries.

GREENE'S AUTO PARTS, Columbus, OH   *Part-time, XXXX–present*
Delivery Person. Prepared orders, developed route, and delivered parts based on faxed and telephone orders. Met or exceeded quota of 20–30 deliveries per day. Provided customer service and researched problems.

RETAIL CLERK, 7-ELEVEN STORES, Walsenburg, CO
January XXXX–present
- Responsible for store maintenance, customer service, cash management.
- Prepared weekly invoice orders.
- Trained new employees.

BELL'S MEATS AND DELI
Butcher. Took orders and served customers. Prepared food and managed the cash register. Assisted with inventory and ordering.

SUNRISE SENOR CITIZEN CENTER
Senior Citizen Helper—Interacted with elderly patrons by playing games, talking, and watching movies. Helped elderly to and from the building, and assisted in general as needed or requested.

JIFFY LUBE
Customer Service Advisor / Upper Bay Technician / Cashier
Specialized in customer service. Certified in preventative maintenance. Supervised two technicians. Managed cash register and sales.

TEACHER'S ASSISTANT - BET YELADIM SCHOOL
Watched pre-school–aged children, prepared snacks, supervised activities, communicated with parents. Assisted teacher with preparing classroom activities and clean-up. Maintained playground facilities and ensured children's safety during play.

BURGER KING – COOK. Prepared food as ordered for busy fast food restaurant; ensured food sanitation. Managed the cash register. Helped with inventory control.

GREAT COOKIE
Cashier: Worked the cash register and waited on customers. Took special orders and prepared cookies. Efficiently restocked inventory.

SERENITY CENTER
Custodial Work—Cleaned dishes, emptied trash and removed to dumpster, vacuumed rooms, and organized objects in the stock room.

MACARONI GRILL
Busser-Cleared and efficiently reset tables. Performed other tasks as requested.

SUMMER YOUTH EMPLOYMENT PROGRAM
Janitor – Cleaned and maintained supplies in washrooms, kitchen, and multi-purpose room. Set up and removed chairs and other furniture for meetings and events. Received 100% attendance award and a $75 gift certificate.

NANNY, The Jones Family, Toledo, Ohio
Planned activities and meals for 3 children, ages 11, 9 and 4. Watched children and supervised their play, making sure they were safe at all times. Planned and prepared two meals per day. Transported children to lessons and other outings. (20 hours per week)

BUNPENNY
Prepared food at popular deli and provided friendly customer service. Efficiently took phone and fax orders and answered questions.

For You

WORK EXPERIENCE

List your part-time and full-time positions. You may need to use additional sheets of paper.

Employer: _____

Position title: _____

Employment dates: _____

Main responsibilities: _____

_____

Skills used: _____

_____

Keywords that would be appropriate for the employer:

_____

Employer: _____

Position title: _____

Employment dates: _____

Main responsibilities: _____

_____

Skills used: _____

_____

Keywords that would be appropriate for the employer:

_____

Putting It Together

In this chapter, you've gathered information you will include in
Now you're ready to start putting it all together. On this page and
page is a Job Resume Outline. Look back at the worksheets in this c
and use the information there to neatly fill in the outline. Do not con.
the Summary of Skills or the Objective sections. Chapters 4 and 8 will
you complete those two sections.

JOB RESUME OUTLINE

_____
Student Name

Street Address _____

City, State, ZIP _____

Phone _____

E-mail _____

OBJECTIVE:

_____

_____

_____

SUMMARY OF SKILLS:

1. _____

2. _____

3. _____

4. _____

5. _____

6. _____

EDUCATION:

Date of graduation: _____

Activities: _____

_____

_____

Honors: _____

_____

_____

Courses: _____

_____

(continues)

WORK HISTORY:

Job title: _____

Company name: _____

Duties:_____

_____

_____

Job title: _____

Company name: _____

Duties:_____

_____

_____

Job title: _____

Company name: _____

Duties:_____

_____

_____

COMMUNITY SERVICE:

Organization's name and location (city, state): _____

    Duties: _____

Organization's name and location (city, state): _____

    Duties: _____

EXTRACURRICULAR ACTIVITIES:

_____

_____

_____

_____

WHAT'S NEXT?

In this chapter, you have listed all the **facts** about your education, honors and awards, activities, workshops and lessons, internships, work-study or co-op programs, technical training programs, community service and volunteer experience, and work experience.

Now you can look at the **skills** you have to offer. Are you creative, outgoing, enthusiastic, hard-working, willing, or good with children? In Chapter 4, you will learn how to list your skills. Get ready!

Describing Your Skills

What Are Students Saying?

I didn't know "talking a lot" was a skill. Now I know it's called "a good interpersonal skill."

Do you want to stand out when an employer considers you for a job? Do you want an admissions person for a college or technical training program to notice you? If so, you will need to let that person know what skills you have. But first you must

- Know what your skills are
- Be able to communicate your skills in writing
- Be able to express your skills verbally

As explained in Chapter 2, both chronological resumes and targeted resumes should include a skills section. In Chapter 3, you listed information about your education, honors and awards, activities, workshops and lessons, internships, work-study and co-op programs, technical training programs, volunteer and community service work, and work experience. In Chapter 4, you will learn to describe your skills. These skills will be included at the beginning of your resume.

If the skills section is the first part of a resume, why weren't you asked to write it first? Why are you creating it now, after writing your list of education and experiences? The reason is that your lists of education and experiences will help you see what your skills are.

Defining the Term *Skills*

Think of skills as being something you do well. In general, skills can be divided in two categories: soft skills and hard skills.

Soft skills. These are skills that are part of your personality, such as being organized or being friendly. Other examples of soft skills are listed later in this chapter. When you are competing with other people for a job, these skills can set you apart. Some organizations such as the federal government look at soft skills carefully. For example, FBI agents must be flexible, willing, dedicated, and hard-working.

Hard skills. These skills may also be called technical skills. Proofreading and computer programming are examples of hard skills. Other examples of hard skills are listed later in this chapter.

Recognizing Your Skills

Pay attention to what people say about you! They can help you begin thinking about your skills and abilities.

Do your parents say you are creative, a good artist, or a computer whiz? Do they say you are a great mechanic because you can fix anything? Do they say you argue persuasively? Do your friends say you are outgoing, friendly, always on time, or neat? Do your teachers say you are hardworking and committed to your practices and homework? Are you patient with younger children or great with school projects? Do people say you are good at science or math? If so, these are your skills. Remember, everyone has skills!

When you look at students' resumes, you can often guess what their best skills are. For example, look at the following "Honors" sections of two students' resumes.

The following student works well with animals and could work on a ranch or in agriculture. He lives in a farming community, so he may have also developed skills such as being dependable, strong, patient, and coordinated.

HONORS
Region 81 Champion Team Roper, XXXX
Rodeo State Finalist (Calf Roping and Team Roping), XXXX, XXXX
Lone Star Farmer, XXXX
Member, 4-H Club—raised show lambs

The following student likes photography and working with children. The student's skills focus on education, recreation, and photography.

Honors
- Honored by Bloomsburg Parks & Recreation Association for outstanding service for volunteerism for early childhood after-school program, XXXX–XXXX
- Received Third Place, Candid Photography Contest, *Washington Post,* May XXXX
- Received a certificate for participation in children's programs, Bethany Baptist Church, XXXX

When you analyze your honors, activities, courses, internships, and work experience, what do you see? Is there a common thread? Are there certain things you do well and enjoy? If so, keep working on those skills and interests. Add to the list whenever you can. That will make an employer more likely to hire you.

When preparing your resume, describe the skills you have gained from your school courses, activities, workshops, lessons, and work experiences. Your descriptions will enable employers to see at a glance what you can do for them.

Employers value skills that can be used in specific jobs, but they also look at the skills that make you who you are. In every industry, employers want workers who are willing to learn and who have good reading, writing, and math skills. They want employees who are good listeners and speakers. They want people who can think creatively, solve problems, and set goals. Employers want workers who are motivated and who work well on a team. Look for ways to present skills such as these on your resume.

Soft Skills

You may not realize it, but you possess many soft skills. Describing your soft skills is a good way to make yourself more appealing in the job market. Soft skills can be divided into two categories, as listed here:

Adaptive skills, also called personal skills. These skills are part of your personality. They help you adapt to different situations. Examples of adaptive skills are

- Enthusiasm
- Honesty
- Maturity
- Physical strength and stamina
- Ability to learn quickly
- Sincerity
- Patience
- Ability to get along with coworkers
- Competitiveness
- Willingness to work hard

Performing in a school play improves many soft skills, including teamwork, public speaking, and creative expression.

Transferable skills, also called general skills. These are skills that can be used in many jobs. Examples of transferable skills include

- Finishing assignments on time
- Working with people
- Being dependable
- Being flexible
- Handling many projects at once
- Expressing yourself through art, music, dance, writing
- Staying organized
- Following instructions

- Paying attention to detail
- Speaking before groups
- Leading a club
- Writing clearly

Some skills can fit into either group. For example, if you are a person who pays attention to detail, that is part of your personality and is an adaptive skill. That skill is also a transferable skill because it can be used in many jobs. You don't need to categorize your skills on your resume, but you do need to include them.

For You

SOFT SKILLS

Make a list of your best soft skills.

_____

_____

_____

_____

_____

_____

Hard Skills

Specific hard (or technical) skills can help you get a job, so they are often referred to as job-related skills. Being extremely clear about your technical skills is important. A potential employer will appreciate seeing a list of these skills.

Keep your technical skills up-to-date. For example, if you list Windows 98 when a newer version of Windows is state-of-the-art, an employer may not consider you. Self-study and training courses will keep you current with the latest technology. Virtually every resume in today's job market should include a list of computer or technical skills. Following are two examples of how this section of your resume might look.

Computer Skills

> Macintosh: Microsoft Word (6 years)
> PC: Windows 2000 and XP, Word, WordPerfect
> Keyboard: 40 wpm

Summary of Skills
Word Processing: Word 2000
Desktop Publishing: Multimedia and graphics
Web site development: HTML and basic Web site development

For You

HARD SKILLS

Make a list of your hard (or technical) skills.

_____

_____

_____

_____

_____

_____

Summarizing Your Skills

The way you present your skills to a potential employer is important. The hiring manager may review your resume for only a few seconds. A well-prepared skills summary may be just what it takes to catch the employer's attention.

All of the resume samples in this book include a Summary of Skills. This section is important for any job seeker, whether a high school student or an executive.

As described in Chapter 2, both chronological and targeted resumes include a summary of skills. Your skills lists should be a combination of hard skills and soft skills.

Several skills summaries are provided here for you to refer to when preparing your summary. The following example is a summary of skills for a student who wants to be a physical therapist. Note that the first five skills are soft skills. The last skill is a hard skill.

Summary of Skills:
Hardworking and work well with others
Customer service and public relations skills
Leadership and organizational skills
Patient and understanding
Good memory and attitude
Good computer skills: Microsoft Word, PowerPoint, Excel

In the following summary of skills, all the skills are soft skills. This is a summary of skills prepared by a student who wants to be a CIA agent.

SUMMARY OF SKILLS:
Good listener
Outgoing/friendly
Energetic and hardworking
Work with people well
Positive attitude
Good sense of humor
Good team member

The following summary of skills was prepared by a student who wants to be a computer engineer. This summary includes both soft and hard skills.

SKILLS SUMMARY:
Outgoing and spontaneous
Good memory and attitude
Friendly and work well with others
Patient and understanding
Web Skills: HTML and Java knowledge
Computer Skills: Microsoft Word, PowerPoint, Internet Explorer, FrontPage

You can also refer to the following skills summaries. Each one shows what the student's objective is. In Chapter 8, you will learn to write your own job objective.

Objective: Editorial Assistant
Summary of Skills
❖   Proofread and edit 8-page newsletter monthly
❖   Follow *The Chicago Manual of Style* for editorial consistency
❖   Review and coordinate article submissions by students
❖   Select photographs and write captions
❖   Effective team member in publishing group

Objective: Secretary/Office Assistant
Summary of Skills
- PC experience using Word 2000 (3 years)
- Keyboarding speed 55 words per minute
- Proofreading skills and coursework in business communications
- Received A's in all business technology and administrative courses
- Organized, efficient, and able to handle pressure

Objective: Bench Technician
Summary of Skills
- Four years of experience working with PCs in computer laboratory and on personal system
- Skilled with troubleshooting PC hardware and software
- Coursework and self-study in Windows 2000 and Windows XP systems
- Experienced in installing and upgrading software, backups, and file management
- Technically adept and enjoy reading computer manuals and schematics

---

Objective: Telemarketer/Inside Sales

Summary of Skills
♦ Three years in theater, both drama and musicals, with leading roles
♦ Received A's and B's in all public speaking and communications courses
♦ Three years of experience in retail sales with extensive customer communications
♦ Articulate, outgoing, and persuasive

For You

A SKILLS SUMMARY

List 5 to 7 skills that you realize you have or that other people say you have. List the ones you think are most important for employers to know. Include both soft and hard skills.

_____

_____

_____

_____

_____

_____

_____

Putting It Together

In Chapter 3, you started filling in the "Job Resume Outline" on pages 55–56, but you didn't complete the Summary of Skills section. Go back to the form now and fill in that section. Refer to the worksheets in this chapter.

WHAT'S NEXT?

In Chapter 3, you learned how to organize your resume to show an employer all of your past experiences, education, and achievements. Here in Chapter 4, your have learned to identify your skills. You studied several examples of how to list these skills on your resume.

In Chapter 5, you will look at information about arranging the various sections of your resume. This is referred to as formatting. You will find some tips in Chapter 5 that will help make your resume attractive and readable.

Formatting
Your Resume

What Are Students Saying?

I liked formatting my resume. It's easy once you know what to do.

In today's world, the Internet and e-mail are major ways to apply for jobs, but many employers still prefer a paper resume. You will need to have both an electronic resume and a paper resume, and you will need to keep both resumes up to date.

If you plan to put your resume in an online database or if an employer requests that you e-mail your resume, you will need an electronic resume that can be copied into the textbox of an e-mail. A paper resume works better for local job searches, for networking, and for making cold calls on local businesses.

Paper Resumes

A paper resume is best if you are mailing your resume to a specific person. Keeping the reader's attention focused on your resume is a challenge. The average length of time a person will spend reviewing your resume is 3 to 10 seconds. People are busy and have short attention spans. You will only hold their attention if your resume is attractive, well-organized, and error-free. If your resume is disorganized or is full of mistakes, the employer will probably just throw it away.

A good layout can enhance the content of your resume. An employer's eye will go to the top and center of the page, so your contact information should be in that position. Put other details (such as your skills section) near the top of your resume to ensure that that information will be read. Information at the bottom may be overlooked. Finally, make the resume headings large. This helps the employer find your relevant information.

The following terms will help you understand the elements that affect the look and feel of your resume. Experiment with these elements to get a look you like and to make your resume fit one page.

Font

Many fonts are available on a personal computer. A few popular fonts are Times New Roman, Arial, Bookman Old Style, and Baskerville. Each type font conveys a different feel and image. Limit the number of fonts you use in your resume.

Times New Roman

This font is very traditional and looks like book type. It is conservative and very easy to read. Times has serifs, which means that the type has edges. Here is part of a resume in Times New Roman:

EDUCATION

Martin High School, Restaurant Management Program, Sacramento, CA; graduated May XXXX

Major Courses

Restaurant Management   Food Preparation and Baking

Purchasing   Computerized Inventory Control

Arial

This font is more contemporary and is sans serif, which means that the type does not have edges (without serif). It is very clean, bold, and rather assertive, as you see in the following example:

EXPERIENCE

Jonelle's Lodge, Sacramento, CA   January XXXX–Present

Chef's Assistant. Assist with food preparation for banquets (25 to 250 guests) and full-service meals. Assist chef with menu planning, buying, and inventory control.

Martin High School Cafeteria Academic years XXXX, XXXX

Chef's Assistant. Assisted cooks with food preparation. Devised improved serving methods for students. Maintained salad bar. Worked as server and dishwasher as needed.

Bookman Old Style

This font is a serif font and has a graphic look. The type is wide and takes up more room than the two fonts above. The bold is very dark. This font looks more distinctive than Times New Roman. Study the following example:

SKILLS and QUALIFICATIONS

- Food preparation, sanitation, menu development and implementation, promotional sales, catering, banquet preparation and service, dining room service, bakeshop production
- Hold California State Sanitation Certification
- Good communication skills; bilingual Spanish/English

Baskerville

This type is a serif font. It is very classy. It is a thin font and not as bold as the others, but it has a regal look. This font makes a resume stand out, as the following sample shows:

EDUCATION

Nottingham High School, Orlando, FL

Allied Health Tech Prep Program–Direct Patient Care. Graduated May XXXX.

GPA 3.963 Rank 2/273

Selected courses: Medical Terminology; Anatomy and Physiology; Biology; Chemistry; Psychology; Spanish I, II, III

Type Style

Bold, *italic*, ***bold italic***, ALL CAPS, and SMALL CAPS are type styles. Be consistent with the use of type style. For example, if you use bold and all caps for one job title, use bold and all caps for every job title. If you use italic for your position titles, do so each time.

Bold

Bold type can be used to highlight major headings, school and employer names, titles of positions, and any other information you want to stand out.

> **Glenelg Country School,** Glenelg, MD

Italic

Latin words, such as *magna cum laude* and the names of fraternities or sororities, are usually typed in italic. Italic type is harder to read, so use it sparingly.

> Graduated *summa cum laude*, XXXX

Bold Italic

Bold italic is useful for secondary headings. A typical use for bold italic would be the titles of positions.

> ***Hostess,*** Edison Assisted Living Center

All Caps

When the type style is "all caps," the size of each letter is the same. Major headings are usually in all caps. Sometimes employers' names and the name of your school can be in all caps.

> EDUCATION
>
> COMMUNITY SERVICE
>
> COMPUTER SKILLS

Small Caps

When the type style is "small caps," all of the word or phrase is in caps. However, the first letter of each word is slightly taller than the other letters in the word. Using small caps is another way to emphasize titles, names, and section headings.

> SUSAN M. GOWER
>
> EDUCATION
>
> WORK EXPERIENCE

Point Size

Point size refers to the size of the letters. Typically, 11-point type is used for most resumes; 10-point is acceptable if you need to fit a great deal of information on one page. You might want to set your name in 14-point type so it stands out. The headings for your resume could be in 12-point for extra emphasis.

> **Tip** This chapter contains formatting guidelines, not formatting rules. Use your creativity to adapt these guidelines to your resume.

Layout

Layout is the overall design of the resume. It includes the placement and alignment of various elements of your resume. Be consistent with your layout. For example, use the same amount of spacing between each section of your resume.

Copyfitting

This means fitting your resume into a certain amount of space, usually one page. You can copyfit by adjusting the space between lines and by changing the type size, type font, and margins. If your resume is 5–10 lines longer than one page, you can copyfit the information into one page by changing the spacing and type.

White Space

White space between and around sections of your resume makes your resume easier to read. However, too much white space causes a resume to look skimpy. Too little space makes it look busy and cluttered. Use your judgment to obtain an easy-to-read mix of words and white space.

Paragraphs

Paragraphs can be written in block style or with bullets to highlight every sentence, as you see in the following samples. Note that the information in each sample is the same.

Stevenson Volunteer Fire and Ambulance Company Summer XXXX

Volunteer Firefighter
    Active volunteer in community, with the duty of providing quality medical care to the sick and injured and preserving life and property.

Stevenson Volunteer Fire and Ambulance Company Summer XXXX

Volunteer Firefighter

    ○   Active volunteer in community

    ○   Provide quality medical care to the sick and injured

    ○   Preserve life and property

Formats

Three resume formats are traditional, contemporary, and graphic. Each conveys a different feel and serves a different purpose.

You will find examples of these formats on the following three pages.

Traditional

A traditional-style resume uses Times New Roman or other serif type that is easy to read.

TERRY R. RICHARDS

25 Esposito Lane
Bakersfield, California 90000
Cell phone: (555) 555-5555   E-mail: trr@aol.com

Objective

Sales Associate—Outdoor Recreation Retail

Skills & Knowledge

* Knowledge and experience in outdoor recreation and parks.
* Firsthand experience with trail construction tools and equipment.
* Communication and instruction skills in use of equipment, tools, and methods.
* Experienced in crew living and camping in the backcountry for a total of 20 months.
* Knowledge of environmental programs and importance of minimum impact camping.

Work Experience

CALIFORNIA CONSERVATION CORPS
CORPS MEMBER/TRAIL WORKER (PAID POSITION) Summer XXXX
KLAMATH NATIONAL FOREST, SHASTA TRINITY NATIONAL FOREST, KINGS CANYON NATIONAL PARK

- Maintained trails, constructed rock work, and rehabilitated damaged meadows.
- Constructed causeway, single and multitier rockwall, inside and outside drains, and wash pans over slickrock and through trail sections that have undergone erosion and water damage.
- Camp life: Lived and worked with 18 people in the crew for four months in the backcountry. Shared kitchen patrol duties; relocated camp frequently; hiked trail and cross-country tours for as far as 20 miles round-trip; attended four classes per week in related subjects.
- Equipment: Crosscuts (saw), picks, pulawskis, sledge hammers, chinking hammers, shovels, loppers, pinonjars, dirt buckets, blasting equipment.

SALMON RESTORATION SPECIALIST (PAID POSITION)   April XXXX–April XXXX
SALMON RESTORATION PROJECTS/FISHERIES AND OIL RECYCLING EDUCATION

- Constructed salmon restoration sites.
- Utilized natural materials to improve the salmon habitat.
- Repaired damaged sections of riparian zones.

Special Skills & Awards

- Presentations concerning environmental effects of oil recycling, XXXX.
- Corps Member of the Month, March XXXX.

Education & Training

Bakersfield High School, Bakersfield, California—Expect to graduate May XXXX.
Other Training: How to Pack for the Backcountry, X/XX, 20 hours; Minimum Impact Camping, X/XX, 20 hours; Basic First Aid, X/XX, 10 hours; River Rescue, X/XX, 8 hours.

Other Interests

Member of soccer team (goalkeeper). Also enjoy basketball, mountain biking, and photography (35mm), in addition to camping and hiking.

Contemporary

Give your resume a contemporary look by using Arial or other sans serif type that is bold and dynamic.

ANDY G. TABORI
108 Cliff Avenue
Reno, NV 99999
Cell phone: (555) 555-0000

OBJECTIVE Seeking an internship in the field of culinary arts and the hospitality industry

EDUCATION Reno High School, Reno, NV. Expect to graduate May XXXX

Culinary Arts and Restaurant Management Program

Major Courses:

Restaurant Management	Purchasing
Food Preparation and Baking	Menu Planning
Computerized Inventory Control	Sanitation

SKILLS Food Preparation, Sanitation, Menu Development and Implementation, Promotional Sales, Catering, Banquet Preparation and Service, Dining Room Service, Bakeshop Production

- Hold California State Sanitation Certification

- Good communication skills; bilingual Spanish/English

- Computer literate (PC and Mac)

EXPERIENCE **Reno High School Cafeteria** XXXX–current

Cafeteria Cook. Assist cooks with food preparation; maintain salad bar; work as server and dishwasher as needed.

Kingsways Inn, Reno, NV Summer XXXX

Banquet Assistant. Assisted with food preparation for banquets and full-service meals. Assisted chef with menu planning, buying, and inventory control. Maintained sanitation in kitchen.

St. Andrew's Catholic Church, Reno, NV Summer XXXX

Handyman. Performed grounds maintenance and janitorial duties.

COMPUTER SKILLS Windows, Printshop Deluxe, Internet

INTERESTS Cooking, camping, skiing, swimming, and fishing

Professional and personal references available on request

Graphic

A graphic resume can make use of lines, shadows, borders, and graphics. Suggested type fonts are Arial, Book Antiqua, or an unusual but readable font like Biffo or Gills Sans.

Anna Marie Symmons

894 Second Avenue / Syracuse, IN 00000-9999 / (555) 555-5555 / AnnaMS@msn.com

OBJECTIVE

A position in the health care field while studying to become a registered nurse.

SKILLS and QUALIFICATIONS

- Experienced in direct patient care.
- Certified in CPR and First Aid by the American Red Cross.
- Certified as a CPR and Emergency Care Provider by the American Heart Association.
- Good communication skills and ability to work well with people.
- Speak, write, and read Spanish.

EDUCATION

Nottingham High School, Syracuse, IN

HEALTH TECH PREP PROGRAM: Direct Patient Care.
Expect to graduate in May XXXX.

Selected courses: Medical Terminology; Anatomy and Physiology; Biology; Chemistry; Psychology; Spanish I, II, III

CLINICAL EXPERIENCE

Summit Nursing Home   September XXXX–Present
        –Nurse's Assistant (10 hours/week)

St. Agnes Hospital
        –Outpatient Center Assistant (20 hours/week)   Summer XXXX

OTHER WORK EXPERIENCE

Carolyn's Florist and Greenhouse, Syracuse, IN   April XXXX–Present
        –Salesperson working extensively with the public; maintain inventory and order supplies; design floral arrangements.

Church of the Nazarene, Syracuse, IN   School Year XXXX–XXXX
        –Religious education teacher for first-grade class (part-time evenings).

COMPUTER SKILLS

PC: WordPerfect 9. Macintosh: Microsoft Word 2000 and Works.

Electronic Resumes

An electronic resume is simply one that you can send by e-mail. When preparing an electronic resume, be sure to emphasize the right keywords. Do not use formatting, indentations, or highlighting in the document. Formatting often will not convert to the employer's computer system and may make the document almost unreadable when the employer opens the file. An employer doesn't want to have to interpret your resume. He or she probably won't contact you for an interview if your resume isn't impressive.

As you prepare and send your electronic resume, remember the following tips:

- Use 12-point type.

- Use all caps for emphasis only.

- Proofread carefully.

- Take all the formatting out of your resume—no indentations, bold type, or underlines.

- Avoid using *I* at the beginning of every sentence.

- Include keywords and skills that will be of interest to the employer.

- Follow the organization's directions for submitting the resume.

- Find out if the company will accept a job application by e-mail. If not, send your resume and letter in the mail.

- Find out if the company accepts attached files. Some companies will not open attached files at all.

- Find out if the company accepts PC, Word, WordPerfect, or Macintosh files. If not, paste your resume in the textbox of the e-mail to be sure it is received.

- If the company is online and an e-mail address is included in the advertisement, e-mail will be the fastest and best way to submit your resume.

- In the subject line of the e-mail, state the job title and your name. For example, the subject line might be "Patient Services Rep—Susan Jones, applicant."

An electronic resume should not include formatting, indentation, or highlighting.

Saving Your Electronic Resume

Here are some pointers for saving your resume onto a disk so that you can easily modify and print it when needed.

- If you keep your resume on a hard drive, you should back it up on a disk and keep it somewhere safe. You should also keep a printed copy of the resume for easy reference.

- Save your resume with a name that tells something about what the file contains. This will enable you to find the file quickly and easily. Include your last name in the file name; for example, troutmancollege.doc or troutmanelectronic.doc. If you send your resume by e-mail and the employer saves it, you want your name to be in the file name.

On page 73 of this chapter, you looked at Terry Richard's paper resume. Here is Terry's electronic resume.

TERRY R. RICHARDS
Esposito Lane
Bakersfield, California 90000
(555) 555-5555

Objective
Sales Associate—Outdoor Recreation Retail; Outdoor Equipment Specialist

Skills & Knowledge

Outdoor recreation and parks experience. Trail construction experience; tools and equipment
use; safety equipment and procedures in backcountry. Knowledge of environmental programs
and minimum impact camping. Member of team. Excellent planning and communications skills.

Work Experience

Summer XXXX
CALIFORNIA CONSERVATION CORPS

Corps Member/Trail Worker (paid position)
Klamath National Forest, Shasta Trinity National Forest, Kings Canyon National Park
Maintained trails, constructed rock work, and rehabilitated damaged meadows.
Constructed causeway, single and multitier rockwall, inside and outside drains, and wash
pans over slickrock and through trail sections that have undergone erosion and water
damage.
Camp life: Lived and worked with 18 people in the crew for four months in the backcountry.
Shared kitchen patrol duties; relocated camp frequently; hiked trail and cross-country tours
for as far as 20 miles round-trip; attended four classes per week in related subjects.
Equipment: Crosscuts (saw), picks, pulawskis, sledge hammers, chinking hammers, shovels,
loppers, pinonjars, dirt buckets, blasting equipment.

April XXXX–April XXXX
CALIFORNIA CONSERVATION CORPS
Salmon Restoration Specialist (paid position)
Salmon Restoration Projects/Fisheries and Oil Recycling Education.
Constructed salmon restoration sites. Utilized natural materials to improve the salmon
habitat. Repaired damaged sections of riparian zones.

Special Skills & Awards
Presentations concerning environmental effects of oil recycling, XXXX.
Corps Member of the Month, March XXXX.

Education & Training
Bakersfield High School, Bakersfield, California—Expect to graduate May XXXX.
Other Training: How to Pack for the Backcountry, X/XX, 20 hours; Minimum Impact
Camping, X/XX, 20 hours; Basic First Aid, X/XX, 10 hours; River Rescue, X/XX, 8 hours.

Other Interests
Member of Soccer Team (goalkeeper). Also enjoy basketball, mountain biking, and
photography (35mm), in addition to camping and hiking.

Whenever possible, e-mail your resume by including it in the textbox. You won't be able to use great formatting, but you won't have to worry about whether the employer will be able to open your attachments.

If you are asked to send your resume as an attached file, use your formatted resume. For best results, use a major word processing program.

Formatting Summary

Here are pointers to keep in mind as you format your paper resume and your electronic resume.

- Do not include your birth date or a photograph of yourself. Equal Employment Opportunity laws state that employers cannot discriminate against people because they are too young or too old.

- Do not include statements about your health, unless you're applying for a physical job.

- Do not include your Social Security number. Give it to an employer on your application, if requested.

- State your objective carefully. An objective is optional but helpful. Your objective should state the type of position you desire. It also may list the skills you want to use. Be careful not to limit yourself with an objective. For example, if you state that your objective is to find an entry-level clerical job, the employer may not consider you for more interesting jobs.

- The average length of resumes, including student resumes, is one page. If your resume is a few lines longer than one page, adjust your type size and margins to fit the information on a single sheet. If, however, you have a long list of employers, internships, awards, and activities, then write a two-page resume. Remember that you are selling yourself. If you have exceptional accomplishments as a high school student, you can use two pages.

- When you send an electronic resume, the length is less important. The resume will be put into a database. The employer won't look at the length of the resume, but at keywords and content.

- Use preferred type sizes. As mentioned earlier, use 11-point type for text, 12-point for headings, and 14-point for your name.

Be sure your resume is error-free. Refer to the dictionary and your grammar books as needed. Run the spell checker on your computer, but be aware that the spell checker won't catch all errors. Spell checkers and grammar checkers miss mistakes in dates, proper names, and titles. Also, these tools cannot spot inconsistencies in format.

Have a friend, teacher, or parent (or all three!) read your resume to make sure the grammar, the punctuation, and all details are correct and consistent. This is extremely important! You can easily miss errors in simple things like your phone number and employment dates.

Use good white or off-white cotton bond paper. Look for quality 20- or 24-pound paper that is 25 percent cotton. Or you can choose a high-grade recycled paper. Paper is available in many colors and styles. Resist wild colors. You need to impress the reader with content, not paper color. You can buy nice resume paper at office supply stores. If you are faxing your resume to employers, plain white paper is best.

If you mail your resume, use an envelope that is made of white or brown paper and that is about the same size as your resume. The resume might be scanned into a database, so it shouldn't be folded. On the envelope, write a brief description of what is enclosed. For example, you might write "Enclosed: Application for Cashier Position."

Use a laser printer if you can. Print resumes as you need them. This also allows you to modify your resume as needed for a particular opening. High-quality photocopying of an original is fine also, although you won't be able to target each resume. Copying a copy is not acceptable.

Avoid writing anything negative. You don't have to tell the employer everything, so don't include the following types of information:

Member, Tennis Team, XXXX–XXXX. Resigned due to injury.	Leave out "Resigned due to injury."
Driver, Papa Johns Pizza, XXXX–XXXX. Reason for leaving: speeding tickets.	Leave out "Reason for leaving: speeding tickets."
GPA: 1.9/4.0	Leave out information about your grade point average unless it is high.

Always be honest in your resume. Do not add things to your resume that aren't true.

Update your resume every six months. Add new courses, workshops, community service positions, honors, activities, and jobs.

Allow for white space on your resume. The usual margins are 1 to 1.25 inches at the top and bottom and on both sides. Between resume sections, allow 1 or 1.5 space returns. Spacing between employer names and job titles can be a full return if space permits. Good use of white space makes a resume easier to read.

Other Important Tips

This section covers common grammar and punctuation errors. If you don't have strong English skills, have someone else read your resume to be sure it is correct and consistent.

Personal Pronouns

You do not have to use nouns or personal pronouns to begin statements in a resume. For example, here's the incorrect way to write the duties of a telemarketer position:

- I received inbound telephone calls and answered customers' questions.
- I searched the computer system and gave account information.
- I followed up and mailed corrected statements.

The following sounds much better. The emphasis is on your performance and skills:

- Received inbound telephone calls and answered customers' questions.
- Searched the computer system and gave account information.
- Followed up and mailed corrected statements.

Here's another example. Do not write your job description this way:

```
Mechanic's Assistant    January XXXX-Present
  • I am responsible for cleaning cars and organizing
    parts.

  • I speak to customers about their car's problems.

  • I schedule appointments.

  • I assist the mechanics with routine preventive
    maintenance.
```

Instead, start each bullet point with a verb. The reader knows that you did this work:

```
Mechanic's Assistant January XXXX-Present

  • Organize and maintain parts inventory

  • Schedule appointments

  • Provide customer services

  • Perform routine preventive maintenance on automobiles
```

Verbs

For the job you have now, start your sentences with present-tense verbs.

Safeway Grocery Stores   May XXXX–Current
Retail Merchandiser

- Receive, price, and stock shelves for dry goods

- Assist with inventory and rotate products

- Provide customer services and information

For jobs you had in the past, start your sentences with past-tense verbs.

Camp Counselor   Summer XXXX

- Counseled and planned daily activities for 15 campers.

  Coordinated more than 10 sports events for campers.

  Coached girls' intramural soccer teams.

  Assisted with kitchen management.

Colons

Using a colon after a resume heading is optional. You can use either of the following examples.

EDUCATION: or EDUCATION

Ampersands

An ampersand takes the place of the word *and*. Ampersands are not appropriate in the body text of a resume. You can use them in headings such as the following:

Writing & Editing

Word Confusion

Some errors can be found only by reading the resume in context. The spell checker often doesn't pick up the differences in words that sound the same. Consult a grammar book or dictionary as needed. Here are some words that are commonly confused.

Contraction	Possessive
they're	their
it's	its
you're	your
who's	whose

Putting It Together

Now it's time to create your resume online. Transfer the information you've written in the "Job Resume Outline" on pages 55-56 to a computer file. Use the formatting tips in this chapter. Leave room to add your job objective, which you will write in Chapter 8.

Create your paper resume first. Then use the Save As feature on your computer to save the resume under another name. Take out all the formatting in that second resume, and you have your electronic resume.

Tip: Print your resume a few times as you work on the formatting. This will let you see how it looks on paper and let you adjust spacing, alignment, type size, and other elements.

Create an electronic master resume file. This is a computer file with complete information about your school and work history. The length of this file may be three or four pages. Use this document to keep track of all the experiences you might want to include in a resume. You can pull information from this file to include in resumes that are targeted to a specific job, college, or training program. You can add information to this file as you gain experience.

For You

RESUME FILES

List the names of the computer files you've created so far that relate to your resume. One example is provided for you.

Name of file	What the file contains
troutmancollege.doc	application I can use to apply for colleges

WHAT'S NEXT?

In this chapter, you have created a resume. It may be your first one. You have learned to format your paper and electronic resumes.

In Chapter 6, you will learn to prepare cover letters, references, and thank-you letters. These are tools you will use with your resume.

Cover Letters, Reference Lists, and Thank-You Letters

What Are Students Saying?

I feel good about describing my skills to other people.

You have almost completed your resume! You will put the final touch on it in Chapter 8. Now it's time to think about some other tools that will make your resume more effective. You will need a cover letter to grab the reader's attention and to introduce yourself. You will need a list of references to confirm and support the information on your resume. And you will need to write thank-you letters to follow up after interviews.

Persuasive Cover Letters

Today's hiring and human resources managers are very busy. They tend to skim through resumes and cover letters instead of reading them closely. You only have a few seconds or minutes to impress them. Without a strong cover letter, your resume may not get a first glance. You must quickly present your interest in the job, your experience, and your approach to looking for work. To accomplish this, write a cover letter that includes a bulleted list of your skills. Include skills that are relevant to the job. You can do this even if you don't have much experience.

In your cover letter, summarize the best of what you have to offer. The goals of the cover letter are

- To get and keep the reader's attention

- To impress the employer with your experience and skills

- To match some of the keywords and skills from the advertisement or company Web site with the skills in your resume and letter

- To show your interest in the company and its customers

- To show that you are dependable, professional, and determined

The cover letter is almost as important as your resume. Use it to highlight experiences that are of interest to the employer. You can brag a little in the cover letter about work or activity accomplishments. Do not be bashful about saying that you were a champion swimmer, had a main role in the school play, or are on the school's baseball team. Potential employers will see you as a person with energy and enthusiasm. Hopefully, they will want to meet you and see if you have the same enthusiasm in person.

To create a professional impression, give your cover letter the same look as your resume. Use the same font and paper. Don't staple your cover letter and resume together. This ensures that the employer will be able to scan your resume and cover letter into a database if desired. Send the letter and resume in a large envelope, and don't fold them.

A good cover letter should contain seven sections. Following is a description of each section.

Your Contact Information

Start your cover letter with your name and contact information and the date. Use the same format and type fonts you used in your resume. For example:

> Kimberly Ann Garrett
> 2989 Smithwood Avenue
> Annapolis, MD 99999
> (555) 555-5555—cell
> kann111@aol.com
> September 29, XXXX

Employer's Contact Information

Personalize the letter with the person's name or company name.

> Mr. Paul Jones
> Supervisor
> Smythe Corp.
> 1900 M Street, NW
> Washington, DC 20006

Salutation

If you are contacting a man, begin the letter with

> Dear Mr. Jones: (note the colon)

If you are contacting a woman, begin the letter with

> Dear Ms. Smith:

If no name is listed in the job advertisement, begin the letter with

> Dear Recruitment Manager:

If you can't tell whether the person is a man or woman, begin the letter with

> Dear M. Jones: (or however the name is listed in the ad)

Opening Paragraph

Here are four types of opening paragraphs. Choose the one that matches how you learned about the position.

Newspaper Ad

You might find a job advertisement in your local newspaper or other publication. If so, you might use an opening paragraph like the following:

> I read your advertisement for a Telemarketer in the <u>Washington Post</u> on September 28, XXXX.

Internet Listing

Another good way to find out about jobs is through the Internet. Here is an opening paragraph you might want to use:

> RE: PATIENT SERVICES REPRESENTATIVE, JOB LISTING 10505
>
> I am sending my attached resume for consideration for the Patient Services Representative position. I found the opening listed on the <u>Baltimore Sun</u> Web site, www.baltimoresun.com. I would like to work for a company like yours where customer service and communication skills are important. I am seeking a position where I can communicate with the public and gain business experience.

Referral

Referrals and leads from friends and family members are great! Always follow up on a referral. This is absolutely the best way to learn about a job and to get introduced. And most employers like getting referrals! They trust the recommendation of a valued employee or friend who states that you would be a good employee. This may save the employer from having to review hundreds of applications.

Here are three sample opening paragraphs for a cover letter based on a referral:

Sample 1. I am sending my resume to you because of a referral from Mike Thomas, an associate in your Annapolis store. I am seeking a summer internship where I can use my communications skills and work with the public.

Sample 2. I was referred to you by Mike Thomas, who is my neighbor. He tells me that you frequently hire dependable, hard-working high school seniors in your telemarketing department.

Sample 3. I was referred to you by Mike Thomas, who is a member of my church and a longtime family friend. I understand you are hiring student interns in your telemarketing department. Mike recommended that I write to you and send my resume for your consideration.

Cold Calling

In Chapter 1, page 6, you read about a practice called cold calling. You may remember that making a cold call means that you contact an employer without seeing an advertisement, without having an appointment, and without knowing if the company has an opening. If you choose this option, you might use an opening sentence similar to the following:

I learned about your organization by researching the Internet. You are also in my neighborhood. I am seeking a summer position from June–August and would like to use my communications skills and work with the public. If you are hiring students, I would appreciate being considered. I will call you soon to follow up.

Your Network

Use your network to get referrals and leads. Talk to people in your network. Tell them what you're looking for. Tell them where, when, and why you want to work. They need to clearly understand your objectives.

Be tactful, but don't worry that you are being too pushy in asking for a referral. This is the way many successful adults get interviews and jobs.

Create a List of Leads

When you get referrals for job openings or potential jobs, use the following format to keep track of those leads. You can use 3 × 5 cards, one for each lead. Or you can keep a list in your computer. Use the following format.

Person who gave me the referral or lead:

Person I should contact:

Person's job title:

Name of the company:

Address of the company:

Person's telephone number:

Person's fax number:

Person's e-mail address:

How my referral knows this person:

Job opening:

Second Paragraph

This is the place to impress the reader with the experience you have that is related to the job. Include your hard (or technical) skills here (refer to page 62). You might word the paragraph like this:

> As my resume indicates, I am active in theater in high school and had important roles in two plays. I am also successful in debate and student government. With these experiences, I can offer you excellent communication and interpersonal skills. I maintain a 3.0 average and work 10 hours per week during the school year. Another skill I can bring to your department is my familiarity with PCs, Windows XP, Word 2000, and Microsoft Office XP. I use the Internet regularly and can keyboard more than 45 words per minute.

Third Paragraph

This is your persuasive paragraph. Include a few of your soft skills (refer to page 60). Use a paragraph similar to the following:

> I would be an asset to your organization because I am energetic, reliable, and cooperative. I want to be the best employee I can be. I am always on time to work. I am reliable, cooperative, and resourceful. I am willing to learn new things.

The Closing

End your cover letter by telling the person how and when to contact you. Express your interest in hearing from the company and thank the employer for considering you.

Close with "Sincerely," followed by your typed name. Leave space above your typed name for your signature. Also, include a line telling what is enclosed with your cover letter. Use the following as an example:

> You can reach me on my cell phone any day after 4 p.m. E-mail is also great. I check my e-mail daily. I look forward to hearing from you soon. Thank you for your time and consideration.
>
> Sincerely,
>
>
> Kimberly Ann Garrett
>
> Enclosure: Resume

Before You Start

Think about the company's products and services. Look at the company's Web site. Read their home page. Read about the services they provide. Could you help the company in some way? Could you sell products or provide customer service? If so, be enthusiastic. Use your cover letter to sell yourself to the person who will read your resume. You are your own best salesperson. You will do this again and again throughout your career!

Cover Letter Samples

The following cover letter was prepared by a student who was responding to an ad she saw on the Internet. The ad was for a Library Assistant. Here's the ad, followed by the sample letter:

LIBRARY ASSISTANT–TECHNO TEEN. HS student with computer skills needed to work with computers and library customers. Must know PCs, Word, Internet, and e-mail systems. Must be patient with nontechnical users. 20 hours/week. $10 per hour. Send resume and letter to King County Library System, 15527 SE 8th Street, Bellevue, WA 98007, Attn: Ms. Snyder. Or send by e-mail to dsnyder@kingcounty.lib.wa.st.gov.

Jennifer Holland
90909 Hollins Ferry Road
Arbutus, Washington 90909
Home: (909) 123-1234
Cell: (909) 999-9999
Email: Jennifer_holland121@yahoo.com

December 15, XXXX

King County Library System
15527 SE 8th St.
Bellevue, WA 98007

Dear Ms. Snyder:

Please find enclosed my resume for the position of Library Assistant, which I found listed on the Internet.

My relevant qualifications include:

- I have previously been a library page and have experience teaching the Techno Teens.
- I know the students and, more importantly, the work that will be required in the computer center.

I would be an asset to your organization because

- I can find books on the shelves twice as fast as the requirements.
- I am good at finding things that do not belong, such as books from other libraries.
- I have good people skills. I am patient with computers and people.
- I can solve computer problems very well.
- I am dependable and a hard worker.

I am available 20 hours per week. You can contact me at home after 3:00 most afternoons. Thank you for your interest. I look forward to your response.

Sincerely,

Jennifer Holland

Enc: Resume

The following cover letter was prepared by a student who was applying for a job at the hospital where her mother works. Her mother gave her the referral.

Reagan R. Ruhnke
3456 Rogers Ford Avenue
Columbia, MD 21045
Home: (301) 999-9999
Cell: (443) 999-9999
Email: Reagan_ruhnke@yahoo.com
July 26, XXXX

Ms. Dorothy Rogers, Human Resources
Howard County General Hospital
909 Bright Seat Road
Columbia, Maryland 90909

Dear Ms. Rogers:

I am submitting my resume for consideration for a part-time position as a Patient Services Representative. I know about the hospital positions and patient services through my mother, Kathryn Ruhnke, who has been a Registered Nurse in the emergency room for five years.

Please find enclosed my resume for the position of Patient Services Representative. My relevant qualifications include:

- I have been preparing for a job as a receptionist.
- I was in Co-Op during my senior year in high school.
- I was Co-op Student of the Month.
- I have worked as a receptionist at Career Connections, where I had various job duties such as helping visitors and answering the phone.
- I have also worked as a File Clerk at Woman's Health.
- I worked for Landmark Staffing Agency for a year. I worked temporarily at several companies, as placed by Landmark.

I would be an asset to your organization because I am energetic, reliable, and cooperative. I want to be the best employee I can be. I am always on time to work. I am reliable, cooperative, and resourceful. I am willing to learn new things.

Thank you for your time and consideration. I look forward to hearing from you. I am available to begin working right away.

Sincerely,

Reagan R. Ruhnke
Enc: Resume

For You

COVER LETTER

In a newspaper or on the Web, look for two interesting ads for part-time or summer work. What experience, hard (technical) skills, and soft skills would you stress in your cover letter if you were applying for these jobs?

Ad 1. Job title: _____

What I would stress in my cover letter: _____

_____

_____

Ad 2. Job title: _____

What I would stress in my cover letter: _____

_____

_____

School friends can offer advice for improving your cover letter.

Impressive Reference Lists

References are an important tool in your job search. Following is an example of what a good reference list might look like. You will give this to a potential employer, so it should match the look of your resume.

Kenny T. Day
1010 Edmondson Avenue
Louisville, KY 22222
(555) 444-4444

References

Janice J. Benjamin, President
New Options, Inc.
2311 E. Stadium, Suite B-2
Mount Washington, KY 22222
(555) 555-0000—Work
Supervisor, Internship, New Options, Summer XXXX

Jane Sommer, Director
Sports Management Department
Smith College
84 Elm Street
Frankfort, KY 22222
(555) 555-0000
Swimming coach, 5 years

Judith Dowd
Paris Country School
Paris, KY 33333
(555) 555-8888—School
(555) 555-9999—Home
Instructor for art history and archaeology; student advisor

Lester Minsuk, CPA
29 Exeter Road
Bardstown, KY 33333
(555) 555-3333—Work
(555) 555-4444—Home
Family friend and mentor for career in finance

For You

REFERENCE LIST

On page 15 of this workbook, you listed three possible references. Now it is time to call these people and ask if they will serve as references. Get complete, accurate contact information for each person. Start your reference list on this worksheet.

Reference 1

Name: _____

Title:_____

Company name and address: _____

_____

Phone numbers: _____

My relationship with this person:_____

Reference 2

Name: _____

Title:_____

Company name and address: _____

_____

Phone numbers: _____

My relationship with this person:_____

Reference 3

Name: _____

Title:_____

Company name and address: _____

_____

Phone numbers: _____

My relationship with this person:_____

Effective Thank-You Letters

Do you want to be remembered after an interview? Sending a thank-you letter is the best way to accomplish this. The thank-you letter is a great opportunity to get your name in front of the interviewer again. He or she will be impressed with your attention to detail. Also, you will have the chance to tell the person how much you appreciate his or her time and how much you like the organization. You can also say that you would like to work for the interviewer's company.

This letter needs to be genuine. Don't make a general statement like "I thought your business looked great." Instead, say something like "I was impressed with how professional everyone was and how customers were well taken care of by your employees."

Employers like to know that you noticed their business, employees, and customers. When you're in an interview, pay attention to your surroundings. Check out the displays, signs, windows, and inventory. Find something you like and mention it in your thank-you letter.

Tip Write and mail your thank-you letter within 24 hours, while your interview is still fresh in your mind and in the employer's mind.

If your thank-you letter is short, you can write it by hand. Use a conservative blank card that you can buy at a stationery store. Write something such as

Thank you very much for your time on Monday. I am very interested in your hotel management training program. I look forward to hearing from you soon.

Usually, you will want your thank-you letter to be a little more formal. If so, use your computer to create the letter. Here is a sample thank-you letter. The fonts and paper stock should match your resume.

Olivia Martine
10309 Arlington Boulevard
Des Plaines, IL 99999
(555) 555-9999
omartine@net.net

July 5, XXXX

Ms. Carol Waters
Manager
Perfect Touch Hair Salon
312 Frederick Road
Suite 782
Des Plaines, IL 99999

Dear Ms. Waters:

Thank you for the interview yesterday and the tour of your salon. Your new expanded salon is beautiful, and the customers seem very happy.

As I said in the interview, I would like to be a retail sales associate for your products. I love cosmetics and fashion products personally and it would be a pleasure to talk about and sell what I so enjoy. I think that I could help you market your products to high school students.

Thank you again for your time. I look forward to hearing from you about the position.

Sincerely,

Olivia Martine

For You

THANK-YOU LETTER

In the activity called "Cover Letter" on page 94, you found two job ads. For one of those ads, imagine that you have interviewed for the position. What information would you include in your thank-you letter to the employer?

_____

_____

_____

_____

_____

_____

Electronic Files

In Chapter 5, you learned the importance of creating and saving an electronic resume file. You will also want to create and save files for your cover letter, reference list, and thank-you letters. Reread the information on page 76 under the heading "Electronic Resumes." The information there also applies to your cover letter, reference list, and thank-you letters.

- If you apply for a job by sending an e-mail, paste your cover letter file before your resume file in the textbox. Or send both your cover letter and your resume as attached files.

- You can e-mail your reference list to the employer later, if he or she asks you to do so. Or you can print out the list and hand it to the employer.

- Print out, sign, and mail your thank-you letter to the employer after you have been interviewed.

- When you save your files, include your name in the file name. For example, you might use the following file names:

troutmanltr.doc	for your cover letter file
troutmanrefs.doc	for your reference list
troutmanthankyou.doc	for your thank-you letter

Putting It Together

Refer to the worksheets and information in this chapter to create computer files for your cover letter, reference list, and thank-you letters.

For You

ADDITIONAL ELECTRONIC FILES

List the names of the computer files you've created for your cover letter, reference list, and thank-you letter.

Name of file   What the file contains

_____   _____

_____   _____

_____   _____

_____   _____

_____   _____

WHAT'S NEXT?

In this chapter, you have learned how to create and save your cover letters, reference list, and thank-you letters. Your resume is your most important job search document, but these other three documents will also help you make a good impression on employers.

In Chapter 7, you will have an opportunity to look at several examples of student resumes.

Student Resume Case Studies

What Are Students Saying?

One new thing I've learned about myself is that I know exactly what to put on a resume. That shocked me.

In this chapter, you will see several student resumes. These resumes reflect the situations and abilities of actual students (the names and faces have been changed). Some of the students have accomplished a lot during their high school years. Some have not. Some of them know what they want to do after high school. Others are not as sure.

The resumes in this chapter will probably not match your situation or plans exactly. But they will give you some ideas about what you can do and how you might organize your resume. With a good resume, you can look for internships, quality community service assignments, or jobs. You can attend job or college fairs and keep track of your high school accomplishments.

Tip Research job information by consulting resources like the *Occupational Outlook Handbook*, published by JIST Publishing. Research Federal job internships by visiting www.usajobs.opm.gov/students.

As you look at the resumes in this chapter, you will see that some of them indicate the student's country of citizenship. One resume also includes the correct pronunciation of the student's name. Even if it doesn't seem right, don't let your name or other people's assumptions be something that keeps you from reaching your goals. Remember that you want to do whatever will make an interviewer feel more comfortable about contacting you. You decide.

Sophomore Loves Music, Dogs, and Volunteering

Melody Kemmer

Melody Kemmer says, "I don't know what I will study in college. I love music and theater, but I also like working with people. My mother's a social worker, so maybe I'll study social work. Or I might want to be a missionary. The things I've done at my church and in other volunteer positions have been very rewarding.

"Also, my dog had puppies last year. I found I really enjoyed taking care of the mother and the puppies. So maybe I'll work with animals as a career. As a junior next year, I'll be taking some college-prep classes and trying to get a better idea of what I'd like to do for my career."

On page 103 is the resume Melody plans to use to apply for colleges. She will use this resume if she decides for sure to go into mission work. (Melody worked with professional resume writer Carla Waskiewicj in preparing her resume. Carla can be contacted at The Resume Place, 89 Mellor Avenue, Catonsville, MD 21228.)

Below is the reference list Melody will have ready to distribute when interviewers request it. Notice that the look of her reference list matches that of her resume. Keep this in mind when you prepare your reference list.

MELODY KEMMER

5301 Altavista Drive
Tucson, Arizona 00000

(000) 555-5555   E-mail: melodyk@com.com

REFERENCES:

Richard Silver, Attorney-at-Law, 208 Long Street, Tucson, AZ 90505
(718) 888-8888

Mr. Walter Estonia, Huntz Junior High School, 333 Altamont Drive, Holton Hills, AZ 90555
(676) 777-7777

Rev. Susan Thompson, 905 Quissen Street, Tucson, AZ 90505
(777) 777-9999

MELODY KEMMER

5301 Altavista Drive
Tucson, Arizona 00000

(000) 555-5555   E-mail: melodyk@com.com

ACADEMIC GOAL:

To attend a college or university with an eventual goal of becoming a missionary or social worker with a non-profit, religious, or international peace organization.

SUMMARY OF SKILLS & EXPERIENCE:

Artistic Strengths & Skills

- Accomplished singer and dancer with three years of private vocal instruction and two years at the Tucson Academy of the Arts with a focus on dance/vocal arts. Currently studying piano.

Performing Arts Achievements

- All District Honors Choir, XXXX; Musical Excellence Award, Choir, XXXX; Wesley Sunshine Singers, XXXX; and Phoenix Singers, XXXX.

EDUCATION:

Southmont High School, Tucson, AZ
Sophomore; expect to graduate May XXXX
College Preparatory Classes–GPA 4.0 in Arts curriculum; 3.8 overall
Courses include Spanish I & II, Art, Choir, Math, and Geography

COMMUNITY ACTIVITIES

- Active in community and non-profit organizations
- Member of church youth group; active in food drives and other endeavors, including Summer of Service (SOS); donated more than 100 hours for community programs; participated in project personally raising $250 to benefit people in third-world countries.
- Cleaned burned houses for fire victims in Show Low, AZ, XXXX

EMPLOYMENT:

Administrative Assistant, XXXX to present (part-time)
Kemmer & Silver, Law Associates, Tucson, AZ
Provide clerical and front-desk support.

Counseling Aide, Summers XXXX & XXXX
Huntz Junior High School, Holton Hills, AZ
Provided secretarial and general office support.

PERSONAL INTERESTS & GOALS

Breed and raise purebred miniature dachshunds.
Enjoy travel and experiencing other cultures and customs. Recently traveled to Sweden, home of my mother's ancestors, as well as extensively throughout the United States.

Junior to Become Airframe Mechanic

Calvin Kline

Calvin Kline says, "I would like to be an airframe mechanic with a commercial airline within five years. I would also like to continue to buy and sell vintage cars. This will give me a good background for working on aircraft. After high school I want to start working toward being certified by the FAA [Federal Aviation Administration]. I enjoy school and learning and particularly like the technical programs. I like to do things with my hands, and I also like my math and English classes. It doesn't take me long to understand new math concepts."

On page 105 is the resume Calvin plans to use to apply for a tech school near his home. (Calvin worked with professional resume writer Carla Waskiewicj in preparing his resume. Carla can be contacted at The Resume Place, 89 Mellor Avenue, Catonsville, MD 21228.)

Below is the thank-you letter Calvin sent following an interview for a part-time summer position as an auto technician. Note that the look of the thank-you letter matches the look of his resume. Keep this in mind when writing your thank-you letters.

CALVIN KLINE
90555 ROCKY MOUNTAIN WAY
FT. COLLINS, COLORADO 80526
(970) 000-0000

December 10, XXXX

Mr. Mark Stevens, Owner
Highline Motors
95000 Mountain Road
Ft. Collins, CO 90555

Dear Mr. Stevens:

I would like to thank you for talking with me on Wednesday about your business and a possible summer position as an Auto Technician. It would be very important for my career to gain hands-on shop experience working on a variety of automobiles.

I learned something about your business just in our 30-minute interview. I realize the importance of quality work along with being efficient with time. I am a good worker, can learn quickly and would enjoy the challenge of taking good care of your customers' automotive needs.

I am available to work Tuesday and Thursday starting at 1 p.m., as well as Saturdays. Thank you very much and I look forward to hearing your decision about the part-time position.

Sincerely,

Calvin Kline

CALVIN KLINE

90555 ROCKY MOUNTAIN WAY
FT. COLLINS, COLORADO 80526
Cell phone: (970) 000-0000   E-mail: calvink@me.com

ACADEMIC GOAL:

To complete my mechanical training and certification.

CAREER GOAL:

To gain relevant work experience using my education, prior experience, and strong technical skills toward my goal of becoming a commercial airframe mechanic.

SKILLS SUMMARY:

Excellent mechanical skills   Welcome challenging projects
Detail-oriented and responsible   Strong technical and diagnostic skills
               Enjoy hands-on technical projects and automotive repair/restoration

EDUCATION:

Rocky Mountain High School, Ft. Collins, CO Class of XXXX

Completed Technical Program, focusing on Industrial Design and Automotive Diagnostics and Repair. **Courses included:** Industrial Physics, Welding, Machining, Drafting, Automotive Drive Train/Heating/AC, and Diagnostics and Electrical.

Honors & Awards:

- Merit Awards in Welding and Automotive
- Accepted at the Emily Griffith Opportunity School's Aircraft Training Center in Denver, Colorado. Expect to graduate in XXXX.

EMPLOYMENT:

Auto Technician	Highline Motors, Ft. Collins, CO - Summer XXXX Repair and maintain high-end import cars.
Installer	Vanworks, Ft. Collins, CO - Summer XXXX Installed leather interiors, running boards, custom electronics, and aftermarket accessories for custom conversion van company.
Craftsman	Wood Shop, Ft. Collins, CO - Summer XXXX Crafted custom dashboards from quality hardwoods and veneers.
Autotech Trainee	Wilf's European Motors, Mead, CO - Summer XXXX

SPORTS / SPECIAL INTERESTS:

Purchase, repair, and sell custom-built automobiles. Projects completed include a 1977 Porsche 930, and a 1976 FJ40 Four Wheeler - rebuilt and restored from the frame up.
Compete in local auto races. Collect and ride dirt bikes.
Won People's Choice Award in local 4x4 show for 1978 Chevy truck.
High school sports include boxing and swim team.

Dual Citizenship: United States and Latvia
Recommendations: Upon request

Sophomore Faces Challenge of Career in Skin Care

Gloria Ramirez

Gloria Ramirez says, "If I relate what I like to do now to what I might want to do for a career, I'd say that I like fashion, beauty products, and salon services!" She adds, "I realize that beauty products are a huge industry and that people are willing to spend money on looking better. Skin care offers great job opportunities."

Gloria is considering training as an aesthetician or hair stylist. "I'm going to start working toward my certification right after high school so I can become skilled to go with a high-quality salon locally or at a resort area. It's important to me to enjoy what I do for a living."

Gloria's resume is on page 107. She can update this resume as she completes her last two years of high school. Then she'll be ready to apply for acceptance into aesthetician school (often called beauty school).

Gloria could consider another part-time job while she's in high school. Or she could ask about internships at a spa or at a makeup and fashion-accessory retailer. Experiences in these businesses would help her get some strong references. They would also look great on her resume and might lead to the career she's looking for.

If you too are interested in this kind of work, here are a few suggestions you might look into:

- Experience Aveda—Concept Salon, Spa, Environmental Lifestyle Stores. Locate an Aveda store where you can work part-time or as a volunteer. Ask about internships. Check out their Web site at www.aveda.com.

- Elizabeth Arden Red Door Spas. Locate a spa and apply for part-time or volunteer jobs. Inquire about internship programs. Check out their Web site at www.reddoorsalons.com.

- Sephora Retail Stores—make-up and fashion accessories. Ask for part-time jobs and internships. Visit their Web site at www.sephora.com.

- Other retailers who specialize in skin care and beauty products: Bath & Body Works, Victoria's Secret, Skin Market, The Boyd Shop, Saks Fifth Avenue.

• Gloria Ramirez •

101 Edmondson Avenue
Springfield, IL 66666
(555) 555-3333
E-mail: gramirez@ari.net

Objective

Skin Care Specialist—Planning to attend aesthetician school to become a Certified Aesthetician.

Skills Summary

Leadership and organizational skills
Customer service and communications
PC skills using Word 2000 and keyboarding 50 wpm
Bilingual Spanish and English

Education

Springfield High School, Springfield, IL
Sophomore; expect to graduate May XXXX

Activities

Sophomore Class Vice-President—School Year XXXX–XXXX
Lead meetings, plan events, fundraising.

Member of Future Business Leaders of America—School Year XXXX–XXXX

Freshman Class Treasurer—School Year XXXX–XXXX
Handled budgets, fundraising, and cash control.

Specialized Training

Merle Norman, Springfield, IL—Spring XXXX
Internship—Advised customers in make-up application. Presented skin care products to customers based on client needs and interests. Gained knowledge and experience in Merle Norman products, skin care processes, and customer relations skills. Received, maintained, and managed product inventory.

Employment

The Perfect Touch, Springfield, IL (15 hours/week)—July–October XXXX–XXXX
Retail Sales and Cosmetics Consultant for Merle Norman Cosmetics.
Assisted with product merchandising, inventory control, displays, and customer service.

Bagel Bin, Springfield, IL (15 hours/week)—March–June XXXX
Prepared sandwiches and operated cash register.

U.S. Citizen

Junior Has Many Interests But Uncertain Objectives

Kylie Jennings

Kylie Jennings says, "I'm definitely going to college, but I'm not sure what I want to major in. After college, I may want to get a graduate degree. I'm not clear about what job I'll get, but I'm sure it will all work out."

Kylie is content to be uncertain of her career objectives at this time. She has confidence that her degree and skills will lead her in the right direction. Her skills are obvious: foreign languages, math, business, and science. After a year or two in college, her career goals will begin to take shape.

Kylie's resume is on page 109. She can use an updated version of this resume later to apply for college admission. Now, she plans to use it to find a student research position.

Following is a list of activities Kylie might want to get involved in while she's still in high school. These activities can give her a better idea of what she does and does not want to do for her career.

If you are uncertain of your education and career goals, you might try some of these ideas, too.

- ✏ Local high school athletic and game coach. Volunteer to coach and assist students with athletic activities and events.

- ✏ Mathematics tutor for disadvantaged kids. Volunteer to tutor younger students in math and science courses.

- ✏ Outdoor leadership counselor. Apply for positions or community service in outdoor leadership schools. Check out the National Outdoor Leadership School's Web site at www.nols.edu.

- ✏ Youth Conservation Corps, Department of Interior (www.doi.gov) or National Park Service (www.nps.gov) volunteer programs. Apply for internships with outdoor programs which will require travel, interpretation, or outdoor skills in summer programs.

KYLIE MARIE JENNINGS

124 Hana Avenue, Haiku, HI • (555) 555-9999
E-mail: bigwave@net.net

OBJECTIVE

Seeking experienced in research in a scientific environment where I can utilize mathematics and science skills and interest before commencing college.

EDUCATION

HALL COLLEGE PREPARATORY, Olinda, Maui, Hawaii - Expect to graduate in XXXX

Academic Courses:	Headmaster's List, GPA: 3.9 (XXXX–XXXX school year)
	Japanese I and Spanish IV
	Honors Physics, Pre-Calculus, and Spanish
Activities:	Member, Cross-Country and Track Teams

WORKSHOPS

Smyth School of Art, Washington, DC, Summer XXXX—Studio Art and Photography
Costa Rica, South America, Summer XXXX—Spanish Language Immersion

INTERNSHIP

San Mateo Research Center, San Diego, California, Summer XXXX
Research Assistant—Assisted researchers with projects to find a cure for diabetes. Administrative assistant with record-keeping; performed basic research duties and computer database updates. Worked with clinical trials staff and patient volunteers.

EMPLOYMENT

MAUI RETAIL CORP., Lahaina, Maui, XXXX to present
Retail Sales/Computer Assistant to the Regional Manager

- Perform computer research concerning inventory, costs, and store information
- Research competitive companies, products, and catalogs via the Internet
- Manipulate online data to create sales and financial reports
- Develop formulas and create Excel spreadsheets, graphs, and reports for management and financial analysis by managers

SKILLS

Languages: Fluent Spanish; currently studying Japanese
Computers: PCs with Windows 2000, Excel, Word, Internet, e-mail

INTERESTS

Extensive travel in the U.S. and South America
Hawaiian culture and history
Philosophy and environmental sciences

PERSONAL QUALITIES

Dependable, hard-working, motivated, sincere, and analytical
Challenged by learning and new experiences

Matthew Manowitz

Junior Enjoys Golf, Looks Forward to Business Degree

Matthew Manowitz had this to say about his future plans, "My school activities and work move around golf. I love the game, the people, and the business. I believe that I will somehow be involved in the golf industry in sales, club management, tournament management, or other aspects of the golf business. I'll be applying for scholarships at universities where there is a golf team."

Matthew's resume is on page 111. He'll use this resume to apply for college and to secure a spot on the school's golf team. (Matthew worked with professional resume writer Carla Waskiewicj in preparing his resume. Carla can be contacted at The Resume Place, 89 Mellor Avenue, Catonsville, MD 21228.)

Following is the cover letter Matthew used to apply for a sports management internship with the Baltimore Ravens. You might follow a similar format when writing your cover letter.

MATTHEW C. MANOWITZ
12605 Grand Mill Road
Owings Mills, Maryland 21136

(410) 899-9998   E-mail: mmgolf002@comcast.net

December 12, 2002

Mr. Thomas Walters
Director, Sports Team Staff Support Recruitment
Ravens Football Team
Raven Stadium
Baltimore, MD 21228

Dear Mr. Walters:

I am submitting my enclosed resume for consideration of a Sports Management Internship with the Ravens. I am planning to pursue a career in sports management and would like the opportunity to work with the Ravens team in an internship.

I can offer you the following skills:
- Computer skills – Word processing, Internet research, Excel reports
- Sporting Events Coordination – Experience in planning and coordinating sporting events
- Promotion and Communication – Communicating with athletes, vendors, agents, and visitors who attend golf tournaments and events
- Inventory and Equipment Management – Ensuring safety and availability of equipment for events

In addition to being an avid golfer, I enjoy the Ravens tremendously. I am a fan and a local Baltimore resident.

My school hours would permit me to work on Monday, Wednesday, and Friday from 1 to 5 pm. I would appreciate the opportunity to become more familiar with the business aspects of sports management. Thank you very much for your consideration. I look forward to your response.

Sincerely,

Matthew Manowitz
Enclosure: resume

MATTHEW C. MANOWITZ
12605 Grand Mill Road
Owings Mills, Maryland 21136

(410) 899-9998   E-mail: mmgolf002@comcast.net

ACADEMIC GOAL:
To attend a college or university with a strong Business Administration program focusing on International Business and/or Sports Management.

ATHLETIC GOAL:
To utilize my experience and strong background in competitive junior golf to become a member of a college/university golf team.

SKILLS SUMMARY:

Articulate and responsible	Proficient in Word and PowerPoint
Enthusiastic team player	Enjoy new challenges
Excellent public speaking skills	Strong interpersonal skills

EDUCATION:
Loyola Blakefield High School, Towson, Maryland
Junior; expect to graduate May, XXXX
College Preparatory Classes – Full honors curriculum XXXX–XXXX
Courses include French II and III, Chemistry, Geometry, Language Arts, and World History

GOLF ACHIEVEMENTS:
Over five years of experience competing in area junior golf in tournaments, including two years in the Titleist Junior Tour, PGA Middle Atlantic Section. Experienced in stroke play and match play. Current USGA Handicap: 7.9. Lowest 18-hole score: 74. Average 18-hole score: 80.

- **Sophomore Year, XXXX–XXXX**
  Varsity Golf Team, position 5/6 on a 10-man team.

- **Freshman Year, XXXX–XXXX**
  JV Golf Team, position 2/3 on a 7-man team. **MIAA Champions, XXXX.**

OTHER SPORTS/EXTRACURRICULAR ACTIVITIES:
Junior Varsity Track Team, 2 years.
Recreational Team Basketball, 6 years.
Volunteer coach for youth basketball program, 2 years.

EMPLOYMENT:
Caddy & Bag Room Assistant
Greenspring Valley Hunt Club, Owings Mills, Maryland   Summers XXXX–XXXX
Food Service Assistant, Glyndon Pool, Glyndon, Maryland   June to August XXXX

Recommendations: Upon request

Tooraj Enayati

Senior Composes Music, Looks Beyond High School

Tooraj Enayati says, "High school was a pain for me. I changed schools three times and could not find the best format for my learning situation. I have Attention Deficit Disorder, and the regular high school classes were boring. My military school (one year) was too rigid. The prep school required too much homework. Finally, I decided to take the GED. I finished the GED in the top 10 percent of the country. My internship and certification program in recording and engineering was great. I know I'll work in the music industry someday, probably as an audio and video equipment operator."

Tooraj's resume is on page 113. He'll use this resume to find an entry-level position in the music recording business.

Tooraj thinks his resume would be stronger if he had additional experience to include. He may consider a part-time job, an internship, or volunteer-community service in any of the following businesses. He knows he'll meet people who might become mentors and provide references. You might want to investigate some of these businesses, too.

✏ Recording studios. Any recording studio may hire part-time workers or offer student internship opportunities. Call the station manager to get information. Check out Omega Recording Studio's Web site at www.omegastudios.com/home.html.

✏ Radio stations. Visit the Web site www.whfs.com/home/index.html. Go to the internship page. WHFS has internships for juniors and seniors in college or vocational schools. You couldn't apply to this station as a high school student, but you might want to contact them to see if they have a community service program.

✏ Record labels. Choose a record label such as Island Records or Epic. Write to the president or producer. Ask if they have internship opportunities, including online internships. They may know of a radio station or recording studio in your area that offers internships for high school students. Check out the Web sites at www.islandrecords.com and www.epicrecords.com.

Tooraj Enayati

555 Pine Lane • San Antonio, TX 21228
Home: (555) 555-9999 • Work: (555) 555-2222
E-mail: enayati222@yahoo.com / U.S. Citizen

OBJECTIVE: A POSITION IN THE MUSIC INDUSTRY

TECHNICAL SKILLS
- Digital and acoustic music composition and arrangement
- Recording and engineering
- Sound system installation in homes and automobiles
- Internet and digital sound
- Excellent communications skills

EDUCATION & TRAINING
Successfully passed GED, XXXX
Manassas Military High School, Manassas, TX, XXXX–XXXX
Glendary Preparatory School, Howard, TX, XXXX–XXXX

Manders Institute, Houston, TX, XXXX–XXXX
Electronic and computer music workshops, including Audio
Production, Sound Engineering, Composition, Digital Music.

Private piano study (4 years music theory and piano performance)

INTERNSHIP
Alpha School of Applied Recording Arts and Sciences,
San Antonio, TX, 12-week program, Summer XXXX
Alpha is a major multi-studio complex with four professional
recording studios. Internship in recording and engineering under
acoustician James Garner. Assisted engineering for KHFS program
"Just Passing Through."

ELECTRONIC MUSIC EQUIPMENT
Home Studio with PC: Digital Sampler ASR 10, Denon 3-head, 2-
track tape deck, NAD 1600 preamp, Nakamichi EQUIPMENTSTASIS
amp, Infinity Ref, Series II; PC with Cakewalk, Mackie 24x8, Alesis
Adat; Tascam DAT MK30II.
Car Stereo: Sony Disc player, Carver 4650 amp, MTX active
crossover, Boston Acoustic 4.0's, Celestion 12" 4 ohm.
Performance: Keyboard, electric bass, various acoustic instruments.

EMPLOYMENT
Washington Music Center, San Antonio, TX, XXXX–XXXX
Keyboard sales and warehouse work.
Entertaining Interiors, San Antonio, TX, XXXX
Residential home theater installation.

GED Graduate Plans to Be Veterinarian

Jacques Revellier

Jacques Revellier never liked high school. He says, "It just wasn't for me. I couldn't find my place there. But I knew what I liked and that was to work with animals. I enjoyed my biology and botany classes, but I had to tolerate the other classes. It was hard. I've found interesting jobs and even an international internship where I gained great experience as a veterinarian assistant. Now that I'm focused on what I like and want, I plan to go to college and then to medical school. I believe I'll be a success in spite of my high school career. I'm pleased with my resume and the skills I developed through my high school years."

Jacques's resume is on page 115. He'll use this to apply for a position as a veterinary assistant. He hopes to do this kind of work until he's accepted into college.

Below, you'll see a copy of a cover letter he sent when applying for the job as veterinary assistant. This may give you some ideas for your cover letters. (Jacques worked with professional resume writer Wendy Enelow in preparing his resume and cover letter. Wendy can be contacted at 119 Old Stable Road, Lynchburg, VA 24503.)

Jacques R. Revellier, IV

121 Robert E. Lee Hwy.
Bristol, VA 21117
(470) 999-8888
jacques4@mindspring.com

November 8, XXXX
Madison Heights Animal Hospital
999 S. Deer Lane
Madison Heights, VA 21117

Dear Doctor & Staff:

I have three months of volunteer experience at a veterinary hospital in West Africa. In this position I learned a great deal about veterinary hospital procedures and general animal care. I also have veterinary assistant experience working in two local vet hospitals in Bristol and Abington, Virginia.

I have worked with a broad range of animals, from dogs and cats to goats to cows. My experience ranges from taking care of pets at the kennel to helping with an autopsy in an African village. I drew blood from animals (and people as well under the circumstances), prepared slides, used microscopes to identify diseases, and helped with a diverse range of animal care activities.

I was delighted to see your advertisement in the *Lynchburg News & Advance*. I am available immediately and thank you so much for reviewing my resume. I look forward to speaking with you.

Sincerely,

Jacques R. Revellier, IV
Enclosure

Jacques R. Revellier, IV

121 Robert E. Lee Hwy.
Bristol, VA 21117
(470) 999-8888
jacques4@mindspring.com

OBJECTIVE: Veterinary Assistant; Veterinary Laboratory Technician

SKILLS & EXPERIENCE:

- Prepared specimens for laboratory analysis and testing. Prepared and stained slides for microscopic testing for specific disease pathogens.

- Skilled in the use of laboratory equipment and instrumentation.

- Observed veterinary surgical and autopsy procedures on both domestic and farm animals. Provided minor assistance as requested.

- Basic skills in collecting blood, urine, and feces from animals and blood specimens from humans. Performed red and white blood cell counts.

- PC experience with Microsoft Word, PowerPoint, and Access.

EDUCATION:

High School Graduate (General Education Diploma/GED) – State of Virginia – XXXX
Attended Thomas Jefferson High School – Bristol, Virginia – XXXX to XXXX

EMPLOYMENT EXPERIENCE:

BOONSBORO ANIMAL HOSPITAL, Abingdon, Virginia   July XXXX to Present
Veterinary Assistant. Work directly with veterinarian to diagnose and treat a variety of domestic animal diseases and conditions. Assist with routine examinations and treatments. Maintain facility, lab, and equipment.

FOOD LION, Bristol, Virginia   March XXXX to June XXXX
Cashier. Fast-paced customer service position in a high-volume retail grocery store.

HO CLINIC, Ho, Ghana, West Africa   August XXXX to November XXXX
Three-month international volunteer assignment in a third-world African nation. Lived in African compound and worked at local veterinary hospital that cared for both animals and people because of their relatively modern laboratory facilities. Acquired outstanding hands-on experience in phlebotomy, hematology, routine and emergency surgical procedures, field autopsies, and general animal health care.

TRI-CITIES ANIMAL HOSPITAL, Bristol, Virginia   XXXX to XXXX
Animal Care Assistant. Worked weekends while in high school. Cared for domestic animals, cleaned kennel facilities, and provided routine hygiene. Coordinated animal drop-offs and pick-ups.

Laura Redden

Senior Seeks Government Clerical Position

Laura Redden says, "I want to find a government position using the skills I've developed in high school. I have really good keyboarding and computer skills. My father is a career military man, and I'd like to be of help to our country, too. I plan to look for a job as an office clerk as soon as I finish high school."

On page 117, you'll find the resume Laura will use to apply for a position as an office clerk with the U.S. government.

Below is some information Laura discovered when looking into government jobs. If you too are interested in government jobs, this information can help you. The federal government has a program called Student Educational Employment. The program has two parts (called components): one for student temporary employment and one for student career experience. Students at all levels of their education, starting with high school, can apply.

Check out the Web site for this program at www.usajobs.opm.gov/STUDENTS.htm.

- ✎ The Student Temporary Employment Component does just what its name implies. It offers temporary employment opportunities for students. These jobs range from summer positions to ones that last as long as you are a student. The work you do does not have to be related to what you are studying in school.

- ✎ The Student Career Experience Component offers you valuable work experience directly related to your educational goals. It involves periods of work and study while you are attending school. You, your school, and the employing federal agency make an agreement. You may be eligible for permanent employment after you finish your education and meet certain work requirements.

Laura E. Redden
2109 Connecticut Avenue, NW, Washington, DC 20006
Phone: 703-444-4444　　　E-mail: laurar0695@com.com
SSN: 000-00-0000

Vacancy Announcement Number:　　SIS-TM285-02
Position:　　Stay-In-School Clerk (Administrative Assistant)
Grade:　　GS-303-01/04
Location:　　Washington, D.C.

OBJECTIVE: Summer Student Job in Government Agency – Clerical / Secretarial

SUMMARY OF SKILLS
- Outstanding skills in written and oral communications.
- Team player; identify needs and fill them.
- 60 words per minute typing.
- MS Word, WordPerfect, MS Excel, MS PowerPoint, Photoshop, Internet, e-mail.
- Telephones (teleconferencing), photocopiers, fax machines, FedEx labels.

EDUCATION
District Heights High School, Washington, DC 20006.
Expect Advanced Diploma, June XXXX.
Currently in top third of class.
- Art AP test score of 4 out of 5. Earned 4 semester hours credit at GMU.
- Member of the National Art Honors Society, school year XXXX-XXXX.

WORK EXPERIENCE
Clerk (Office Automation), GS-303-2/3
Feb.–May XXXX, 30 hrs/wk—July–Aug. XXXX, Dec. XXXX–Jan. XXXX, 40 hrs/wk
U. S. Department of Transportation, Federal Highway Administration, Office of Human Environment
400 Seventh Street, SW, Washington, DC
Supervisor, Christopher Smith, 202-333-3333

Student Temporary Employment Program (Step) Intern. Office Assistant for Assistant to the Director and professional staff members. Provided computer support— PowerPoint presentations, scanning, research, document preparation. Typing 40 wpm, correspondence, memoranda, papers, and reports. Used Microsoft Word. Special assignment: Finalized response to a congressional inquiry. Assembled, organized, and mailed packages by most cost-effective means. Prepared materials for meetings. Copied materials onto CDs. Scanned documents for electronic filing and retrieval. Answered phone calls, provided customer service, made appropriate referrals. Won cash award of $100 for superior performance during summer internship, Aug. XXXX.

OTHER INTERESTS:
- Second Place in Adult-Youth Bowling Tournament., Jan. XXXX.
- Fifth Place in Adult-Youth Bowling Tournament, Dec. XXXX.
- Won Fire Safety Poster Contest for Camden County NJ (First Place) and went on to state competition, May XXXX.
- First Team All-Conference Female, South Jersey, 6th-ranked female bowler, Feb. XXXX.

David Pastorelli

Junior Athlete Plans Career as Radiologic Technician

David Pastorelli enjoys sports and is a disciplined team player. However, he doesn't plan to make sports part of his career. He wants to work with hospital patients as a radiologic technician. David says, "I do plan to participate in sports while working on my two-year associate's degree. But I really enjoy the sciences, especially the hands-on lab work. I speak Spanish, so maybe I'll work in a culturally diverse area. I like the idea of helping patients feel comfortable in unfamiliar surroundings. I also like computers and Internet IMing my friends in real time."

On page 119 is David's resume. He can use this resume when applying for two-year healthcare programs. He can also use it to get a job or an internship while he's in high school. (David worked with professional resume writer Janet Ruck in preparing his resume. Janet can be contacted at 5620 Mirrorlight Place, Columbia, MD 21045.)

Since David is interested in a healthcare career, he could consider applying for an internship or getting involved in community or volunteer service. He could also get a part-time job in a hospital, medical practice, or Veteran's Hospital (a federal agency).

Here is a list of possibilities to consider if you are interested in a medical career:

- Hospitals. Hospital Web sites usually give lots of information about volunteer training and events. But they may not provide any specific information about how to apply for volunteer positions. They do provide telephone numbers. You can call the human resources office and ask about volunteer opportunities. One example of a hospital Web site is the one for Howard County General Hospital at www.hcgh.org.

- Radiology or ambulatory healthcare clinics. Use your telephone book to look up radiology centers near you. Call the human resources manager and ask if they offer internships, part-time jobs, or community service opportunities. Tell them about your career objective. Maybe they will create a volunteer position or internship just for you. This will help build your resume.

- Nonprofit healthcare associations. The American Red Cross, United Way, and other nonprofit organizations always need volunteers. You could gain experience in administration and special-program support.

- U.S. Department of Health and Human Services. Check out their Web site at www.hhs.gov.

David Pastorelli
31220 Lawyers Hill Road, Elkridge, MD 21777
Home: (401) 555-4444
E-mail: david0654@aol.com

Objective:
Radiologic Technician—Planning to attend a two-year certification program.

Summary of Relevant Skills and Experience:

Writing and Research Experience
Skilled researcher in many of the basic classes, such as Biology, Chemistry, and many different types of language arts. Three years of advanced English classes, which involved many research papers and language development skills.

Computer Skills
Completed two year-long courses of computer applications. Skills in all the Microsoft programs such as Microsoft Word, Access, Excel, and PowerPoint. Experience with PCs, Macintosh, Internet; very good typing skills.

Foreign Language Skills
Three years of high school Spanish.

Education:
Oakland Mills High School, Columbia, MD. Expect to graduate in XXXX.

Academic Honors:
Honor Roll, average GPA 3.4, XXXX–present
Honors English and U.S. History
Student Athlete Award—3 years, 3 sports
Member of the Alpha Achievers, an academically based group

Activities:
Varsity Football and Lacrosse
Junior Varsity Basketball
Member of Black Student Achievement Program (BSAP)

Volunteer Experience:
Christmas in April—Assisted low-income residents with home renovation, April XXXX
Supreme Sports Club—Housekeeping duties—Summer XXXX

Workshops:
Howard Community College: Business workshop and note-taking workshop.

Senior Seeks Summer Job in Government Agency

Danielle Edgington

Danielle Edgington says, "I'm very comfortable in an office environment. I also enjoy sports. I like the discipline of the military and plan to join the U.S. Navy, but I don't want to make this my career. Joining the military would give me a chance to serve my country while getting computer experience and training. I can use what I learn to get a job as a computer operator after my military service."

Danielle's resume is on page 121. She can use this resume to find a summer job before signing up for military service. (Danielle worked with professional resume writer Cory Edwards in preparing her resume. Cory can be contacted at Partnering for Success, P.O. Box 650042, Sterling, VA 20165-0042.)

Below is a list of internship ideas Danielle might consider. You may be interested in these opportunities, too.

✎ Student internship in any federal agency or military base. Use the telephone book to find the name of a federal agency in your area. Find the telephone number for the human resources office. Call the number and ask for information on student internships. This information is not easily accessible through the Internet. Student internships in government are paid and can lead to permanent jobs.

✎ Corporate internship. Find corporations and businesses with headquarters near you. Call the human resources office and ask about student internships, part-time jobs, or community service. These student jobs are not usually advertised. You will need to call and ask what is available.

✎ Federal Bureau of Investigation. Check out their Web site at www.fbi.gov.

✎ United States Navy. Visit their Web site at www.navy.mil.

Danielle N. Edgington
109 Colleen Road
Alexandria, Virginia 20165
(703) 888-0888
email: danielle@yahoo.com

OBJECTIVE: To join the U.S. Navy, developing a career in administration and office-information technology.

SUMMARY OF SKILLS

- Clerical: File maintenance, office administration, mail management
- Computers: MS applications, Microsoft Word, keyboard 55 wpm, data entry, Internet
- Organization: Follow through on details, event planning and coordination
- Communications: Telephone, customer services, team leadership
- Personality: Friendly, quick learner, dependable, hard worker

EDUCATION
- Calvary Temple School, Sterling, Virginia, Graduate Class of XXXX
- GPA 3.0
- Varsity Basketball
- Drama Teams

WORK EXPERIENCE
Various jobs as child care provider, house and pet sitter, house cleaning, wedding planner's assistant, and office assistant.

VOLUNTEER WORK
- Facility Maintenance—Volunteer worker on church and community beautification days. Member of team to provide lawn and garden landscaping and cleanup.

- Special events organizer—Volunteer coordinator for birthday and anniversary celebrations. Plan activities, schedule other volunteers, and organize events. Coordinated several events with more than 100 people in attendance.

- Teacher's Assistant, Calvary Temple Preschool—Work with art teacher to manage children and activities.

OUTSIDE INTERESTS
- Youth group activities
- Youth choir

Siphiwe Mikhize

Senior Sets Sights on Mechanical Engineering Degree

Siphiwe Mikhize talks about his future career: "I'm good in math and science. They're easy for me. I don't know exactly what I will do in mechanical engineering, but I like to design equipment. I might work with military agencies in retrofitting parts for aircraft, helicopters, or vehicles. I hope to attend University of Maryland, College Park as an engineering major."

On page 123 is Siphiwe's resume. He can use this resume when he applies for an internship during his senior year.

Below is the cover letter Siphiwe will use when submitting his resume to the U.S. Army Corps of Engineers. When you prepare your cover letters, remember that the appearance of the letter should match the appearance of your resume. Siphiwe's cover letter is a good example of this.

Siphiwe F. Mikhize
(pronounced Siph-ie Mik-hiz)

105 Rollingwood Road   Home: (410) 555-4444
Ellicott City, MD 21042   E-mail: Mikhize22@com.com

November 20, XXXX

Mr. Sam Smith, Student Recruiter
U.S. Army Corps of Engineers
1005 Lombard Street
Baltimore, MD 21229

Dear Mr. Smith:

I would like to be considered for an internship position in Engineering during my senior year. As you can see from my resume, I have aptitude and skill in advanced mathematics, including statistics and calculus.

I would like to gain hands-on experience in an engineering division where I can support engineers and administration in projects. I am hard working, organized, and detail oriented. I have worked for a family business for several years throughout high school, but I would like an industry internship before beginning college. My communications skills are excellent in performing field work and working with engineers.

I am available to work 20 hours per week throughout my senior year. It's possible that I could work throughout my college coursework since I will be attending University of Maryland, College Park.

Thank you for your time and consideration. I am available for an interview at your convenience.

Sincerely,

Siphiwe F. Mikhize

Siphiwe F. Mikhize
(pronounced Siph-ie Mik-hiz)

105 Rollingwood Road
Ellicott City, MD 21042

Home: (410) 555-4444
E-mail: Mikhize22@com.com

OBJECTIVE: MECHANICAL ENGINEER

EDUCATION:

Centennial High School, Ellicott City, MD, Class of XXXX

Academic Honors:
Honor Roll   XXXX–XXXX
Cumulative GPA: 3.6 / 4.0   XXXX–XXXX
SAT: 700(V) 710(M)
PSAT: 730(V) 730(M) 770(Writing)
National Merit Finalist/Scholar
AP Scholar with Honors

Significant Courses:
Gifted and Talented English, Social Studies,   XXXX–XXXX
Math, and Science coursework
AP courses: Statistics, English 12, U.S. History,
Calculus One and Two, and Psychology.

INTERNSHIP AND COMMUNITY SERVICE:

U.S. Army Corps of Engineers, Baltimore, MD, Sept. XXXX–June XXXX

Engineering Assistant to engineers on projects such as Inner Harbor dredging and Chesapeake Bay environmental assessments. Utilized CAD skills and interpreted specifications. Updated blueprints and charts. Recorded notes for meetings in the field with civil engineers and general contractors.

WORK EXPERIENCE:

Manager, Village Antiques, Oella, MD   XXXX–XXXX
Responsible for customer service, sales, daily operation of store. (18 hours per week)

COMPUTER SKILLS:

Windows 2000, Microsoft Word, Microsoft Excel, Microsoft PowerPoint, Pro-Engineer CAD software, Matlab, Mathematics

U.S. Citizen

Kwan Tak-Hing

Senior Moves Toward Career in Business and Industry

Kwan Tak-Hing says, "I've been putting off thinking about a career, but now it's time. I think the most important thing is to never give up looking for something and trying different opportunities. I plan to look for job advertisements in the newspaper and on the Internet. I'm also considering an internship. I'll probably follow in my family's footprints and find a career in business."

On page 125 is Kwan's resume, which can be used when he applies for a job or an internship.

Below is the cover letter Kwan plans to include with his resume when he applies for a job in a nearby grocery. His letter may give you some ideas of what to include in your cover letters.

Kwan Tak-Hing
4404 Allison Drive
Baltimore, MD 21229
(410) 999-9999 / Chu272@aol.com

September 19, XXXX

Mr. Johnson
A-1 Grocery
246 Story Drive
Baltimore, MD 21229

Dear Mr. Johnson:

I am a senior at Catonsville High School, and I am very interested in the cashier position as stated in *The Sun* on September 28, XXXX. I am very sure that I am qualified for this position.

I have experience working as a cashier and in other positions in my family's business. I can help your business grow. I am a kind person who is excellent at customer relations. I am also a hard worker who follows the instructions with respect. I am well organized with good follow-through. Serving customers is my number one priority.

I have been learning in my business class how to assist customers, how to think the way they think, and how to help them find what they need. I always strive for customer satisfaction. You may contact me at (410) 999-9999 after 2:30 or anytime on Saturday. I am sure I am a good employee, and I hope you will consider my application.

Sincerely,

Kwan Tak-Hing
Enclosure

Kwan Tak-Hing

4404 Allison Drive
Baltimore, MD 21229
(410) 999-9999 / Chu272@aol.com

OBJECTIVE:

BUSINESS: Seeking entry-level positions in a retail or service business where I can gain experience in business operations and management.

BUSINESS SKILLS:

Excellent communications and customer service skills
Attention to detail and organizational skills
Hard-working and able to learn quickly
Knowledge of business operations

EDUCATION:

Catonsville High School, Catonsville, MD 21228
Senior, expect to graduate May XXXX
Significant courses: Biology, World History, English 11

BUSINESS COURSES:

Keyboard 50 wpm
Business Communications

ACTIVITIES

Computer research
Basketball Team

COMMUNITY EXPERIENCES

Church activities—youth programs, physical maintenance services

WORK EXPERIENCE

Tak-Hing Grocery Center, Baltimore, MD, three years
Cashier, Merchandiser, Cook, Inventory Control, and Clean-up at a family-owned and -operated business operation. Gained experience in operations, purchasing, customer service, and merchandising.

Roberto Mendez

Senior Takes His Place in a Family of Tradesmen

Roberto Mendez is from a family of trades professionals. His father, grandfather, and uncles are all maintenance mechanics, pipefitters, and carpenters. Roberto says, "I want to go into an apprenticeship program so I'll be free to relocate and work in many cities. After I finish trade school and complete my apprenticeship, I'll be a certified heating and air conditioning mechanic. Most construction firms are interested in people with my skills. I may decide to apply for jobs at military bases where I can work on airplanes, helicopters, weapons, and other equipment."

On page 127 is Roberto's resume, which he plans to use after completing his apprenticeship.

Following is a list of other internships, work-study, and part-time jobs Roberto could have considered. If you are interested in this kind of work, you might check out these opportunities, too.

- ✏ Aberdeen Proving Ground in Aberdeen, Maryland. This is an army base where there is a large equipment-maintenance department. Student internships are paid and give students a chance to develop excellent equipment skills.

- ✏ Phillipsway, Inc., in Owings Mills, Maryland. This is a general contracting firm specializing in the maintenance and repair of schools and other institutions in Maryland. A part-time job as maintenance assistant would be great experience to include in your resume.

- ✏ State-sponsored apprenticeship programs through your school's community service office. They can give you information on the apprenticeship training organizations and companies in your local area.

ROBERTO T. MENDEZ
1564 Deer Creek Road, RD 1
Philadelphia, PA 17349
Cell phone: (717) 235-555   E-mail: rmendez@aol.com

OBJECTIVE   Seeking professional Heating and Air Conditioning Mechanic positions following completion of apprenticeship.

EDUCATION / TRAINING

Catonsville High School—Graduation Date XXXX
Western Vocational Technical Center, Baltimore, MD XXXX

EQUIPMENT TRAINING:
<u>Sheet metal equipment</u>: Vertical milling machine, steel shaper, steel cut-off-saw, drill press, hand shear and notcher, pipe threader, saw-zall, engine lathe, surface grinder, band saws, steel shear, brake, punch, circle nibbler, grinder, air tools.
<u>Welding</u>: Mig, electrode, spot, tig, carbon arc, gas welders. Burning, plasma arc cutter.
<u>Types of welds</u>: Vertical up and down; Tig & Mig stainless and aluminum.
<u>Miscellaneous</u>: Yoder steel tubing mill; fork-lift operator; large overhead monorail crane; maintenance of tractor-trailer, vehicles, and forklifts.

Computer Aided Drafting Courses: Computer drawing, engineering drafting, architectural drafting for interior design, and architectural drafting.

APPRENTICESHIP

Evapco Air Conditioning, Inc., Taneytown, MD   Part-time two years; full-time summers
Welder / Maintenance Mechanic / Heating and Air Conditioning Apprenticeship
Welded small parts in sub-assembly stage for large evaporative and condensing cooling towers. Designed time-saving jigs for assembling sub-assemblies.
Performed required minor repairs to production equipment. Assisted with preventive maintenance program. Trained in Safety and Occupational Safety & Health Standards.

INTERNSHIPS

Tester/Development Technician, Prototype Pepper Picker,
Kremmer Pepper Picker Manufacturers, New Mexico and Texas   Summer XXXX
Helped to test, demonstrate and evaluate the performance and quality control of mechanical pepper harvester in New Mexico.

PART-TIME JOB

Govary Mining Company, Atlantic City, WY   Summer XXXX
Mechanic's Helper. Operated and maintained rock crushing equipment. Operated loader to bring gold ore to rock-crushing mill. Operated Ford Loader, 1934 D-8 Caterpillar 440-volt generators. Brought equipment up to operating condition.

INTERESTS
Mechanics involving automobiles, boats, three-wheelers.
Also freelance auto repair, equipment repair and maintenance, construction projects.

Senior Enjoys Leadership and Computers

Nathan Brown

Nathan Brown's father is in the U.S. Air Force and is stationed at Ramstein Air Base in Germany. Nathan says, "I've traveled a lot and have attended ten schools in the U.S. and Europe. I guess you could say I'm used to the international lifestyle. I want travel to be part of my career, too. I really enjoy my friends and activities on the base and in the nearby town of Kaiserslautern. I enjoy using my German-language skills. I like outdoor activities and being a leader in the ROTC program. I plan to join the Air Force like my dad. I plan to work in the computer field after I get some additional training."

Nathan's resume is on page 129. This is a resume he can use to apply for summer jobs, internships, or additional training.

Following is a list of summer jobs and internships Nathan may apply for. If you are interested in getting additional training and then enlisting in the military, you might be interested in these opportunities, too.

- ✏ A local park or public recreation center. These jobs offer students experience working outside with recreation equipment. They also provide an opportunity for learning to work with people.

- ✏ National Outdoor Leadership School in Lander, Wyoming. Back in America, Nathan could consider an outdoor leadership program such as the one listed here. Visit the following Web site for more information: http://www.nols.edu/.

- ✏ Outward Bound Programs. Programs involving outdoor leadership, teamwork, and skills development are sponsored by Outward Bound. Check out their Web site at http://www.outwardbound.org/.

NATHAN T. BROWN
1000 Aircraft Place
Ramstein, Germany 00000
(970) 000-0000   nathan.brown@you.com

OBJECTIVE:

To join the U.S. Air Force as a military professional in information technology after completing additional training.

SKILLS SUMMARY:

Analytical skills	Schematic readings and manuals
Self-taught in some computer skills	Strong technical and diagnostic skills
Communications skills	Keyboarding skills: 40 wpm

EDUCATION:

Ramstein High School, Kaiserslautern, Germany   **Class of XXXX**
The Computer Service and Repair Program, (CSS)
Courses include building and troubleshooting computers; Windows; software installation

Work-Study Program:
- Serve as a troubleshooter, make repairs. Provide user support at Kaiserslautern High School and student computer laboratories.

Activities:
- JROTC Member; Recognized for leadership and outstanding attendance award
- Junior Reserve Officer Training
- Member, Wrestling Team, XXXX to present
- Corps Drill Team

Honor:
- Merit Awards in Intro to Computer and Windows XXXX Course

EMPLOYMENT:

Cashier	**AAFES, Mega Power Zone (Electronics) and Front Line Sports Store** Kaiserslautern, Germany, Summer XXXX Customer Service and Inventory Control; Retail Sales
Computer Repair	**Freelance,** Ramstein and Vogelweh Air Bases, XXXX to present Troubleshoot, make repairs, and assist with training in Windows, Word, and e-mail programs for friends and family
Electronics Set-Up Assistant	**Ramstein Air Base,** Facilities Services, Summer XXXX Grounds maintenance, event setup, electronic equipment setup

ACTIVITIES:

Summer Camp Counselor, The Ramstein Community Center, Kaiserslautern, Summer XXXX
Planned activities and crafts for children ages 6 to 12 in small groups

Member, The Ramstein Southside Fitness Center

LANGUAGES AND TRAVEL:

Speak German moderately. Traveled throughout Europe for four years during summers and holidays. Experienced with cross-cultural environments. Enjoy military history and war game scenarios and simulation systems.

Job Search Tips

What Are Students Saying?

I have special skills that can help me find jobs I'm interested in.

Have you started thinking about getting a job—maybe a summer or part-time job? You probably need to make money and get work experience. You may be wondering what kind of job to look for and how to go about finding a job. This chapter will answer some of your questions.

Types of Jobs

Jobs can be grouped into two categories: cash jobs and career-related jobs. A cash job is one you might take just to make extra money. A career-related job is one you select because it helps you develop the skills needed in a specific industry.

As you think about getting a job, ask yourself these questions:

- Do you just want to make money during school or your summer vacation? If so, look for any cash job.

- Do you want to get experience that will help you in a certain career? If so, look for a job related to that career.

These are important questions. Your answers determine what kind of job search is best for you. No matter what kind of job you are looking for, you need to know how to search for a job. In Chapters 1–7, you've already been introduced to some tools and information that will help you find a job. This chapter will give you some additional tips.

Cash Jobs

This kind of position may or may not improve your technical skills for the career you have in mind. But interviewers will be impressed that you have a job. In any job you have, you can learn soft skills such as showing up for work and communicating with people.

Looking for a cash job is fairly easy. However, you do have to be determined. You have to stick with it and be able to handle rejection. Many employers will tell you they are not hiring.

If You Want a Job in the Area Where You Live

If you're looking for a cash job near where you live, here's what you must do:

- Go personally to the company to obtain a job application and to ask if they are hiring. Be sure you look good when you go. The hiring manager might see you right then.

- Ask the person who gives you the application how the hiring process works. Ask if someone will call you for an interview and how long this usually takes. Remember that the person you are talking to may say something about you to the interviewer. If you make a good impression on that person, he or she will have good things to say, and that might get you an interview.

- If the company is taking applications, you can carefully fill one out while you are there or take one with you and fill it out at home.

- Whether you fill out the application when you pick it up or fill it out at home, attach your resume with more details of your experience. The hiring person will be impressed with this.

- If you fill out the application at home and take it back to the company later, remember that you still need to have a neat, clean appearance. You might be asked to interview right then. Be ready.

- Be aware that you may also be asked to fill out an in-depth questionnaire and provide references.

If You Want a Job Outside the Area Where You Live

Here's what you must do if you want to be considered for a cash job that is out of your local area:

- Send your resume by mail or e-mail.

- Follow up by telephone or e-mail to be sure your resume was received.

- Ask what the company's schedule is for deciding on summer hires.

- Be prepared to be interviewed on the telephone by the hiring person or business manager.

Career-Related Jobs

You may want to search for a job with career potential. You may want a job that will help you develop skills you can use in the career that interests you. This type of position impresses hiring managers and college recruiters because it shows that you have experience in a certain industry.

If You Know What You Want

You are lucky if you know what career you are interested in and what skills you hope to use in the future. If you know what career you will someday be seeking, then you should definitely try to get work experience that relates to that career. Here are some tips.

- Find out about the companies that are in your local area or in the area where you want to live. You can do this by just driving around in your area or by using the Internet.

- Look up companies on the Internet. Research their mission, services, and customers. Also, look to see if the companies you are interested in have placed employment ads for summer jobs, internships, or part-time jobs during the school year. If so, write or send an e-mail to the person who is listed in the ad. Submit your cover letter and resume.

- Find other companies that appeal to you because of your skills and career interests. Keep contacting companies, following up, and sending cover letter and resumes.

If You Don't Know What You Want

You may not have decided on a specific career, but you still want to get experience that would be helpful to you. Think about what you like to do, including sports and school activities. Choose one related career that might interest you. By working in one field for the summer or on a part-time basis, you may determine whether a certain career is right for you.

See your guidance or career counselor at school. He or she will have a career and interest test that can help you identify your skills and interests. This kind of test can help you tremendously and can give you great ideas about careers.

Here are some ideas of the types of jobs you could search for, based on your current interests:

- **Arts, Entertainment, and Media.** If you like to draw, paint, or use computer graphics, you could look for work in an art museum, newspaper layout department, print shop, or graphic design firm. If you like to write, you could work for a publisher, marketing firm, or printer. You could look for a company where you could help write or edit a newsletter.

- **Science, Math, and Engineering.** If you are concerned about the environment, you could look for work at a nearby nature center or park. You could contact businesses in your area that deal with recycled materials. If you are interested in science, math, engineering, or technology, you could contact businesses in your area that do scientific research or testing.

- **Plants and Animals.** If you have a green thumb and enjoy working with plants, look for work at a landscaping firm, greenhouse, flower shop, gardening center, or tree farm. If you like animals, you could search for a job at an animal hospital, race track, pet store, or grooming shop. You might find work on a farm, or you might be a pet-sitter.

- **Law, Law Enforcement, and Public Safety.** If you want to work in law enforcement, you could look for jobs in parks, volunteer fire departments, law firms, bonding agencies, or courts. You also might consider intern positions with the Department of Homeland Security and other departments of the federal or state government related to law enforcement and public safety.

- **Mechanics, Installer, and Repairers.** If you like to fix cars, you could get a position in an automotive shop or dealership. If you love airplanes, you might apply for a job at a local airport. If you are interested in military vehicles, you might apply for a student position at a nearby military base, possibly with a stay-in-school program.

- **Construction, Mining, and Drilling.** If you enjoy working with your hands or working outside as part of a team, you may want to look for a job with a home or commercial builder. You also might enjoy working on a road construction crew.

- **Transportation.** If you are interested in the transportation of people, you might want to look for work with a local taxi or bus company. If you are interested in the transportation of materials, you might apply at a nearby warehouse.

- **Industrial Production.** If you enjoy concrete tasks and organized activities, you might want to find a job at a local factory.

- **Business Detail.** If you enjoy indoor work and like organization and detail, you might apply for a part-time job as a receptionist or office worker with a company in your area. You might also want to look for a job in which you can learn about finances, buying, sales, and preparation of reports.

- **Sales and Marketing.** If you love clothes and shopping, you should look for work in a retail store where you can learn how the store managers select their merchandise, manage inventory, and buy seasonal merchandise. If you are a good speaker, like to talk, and are outgoing, you could probably find a job in sales in a local shop or department store. You might also consider a telemarketing job.

✐ **Recreation, Travel, and Other Services.** If you enjoy planning parties and school events, you could apply for jobs with public relations firms, radio stations, or hotels. If you enjoy fashion, beauty products, and sales, you might find work in a hair salon or beauty spa.

✐ **Education and Social Service.** If you like kids and have patience, you could look for a job at a day care center, camp, or swimming pool. You could also apply to the local parks department and the YMCA.

✐ **General Management and Support.** If you are a natural with computers and enjoy helping people solve their computer problems, look for work in a small business, retail computer store, or library. You might also find a position with a company that provides computer services and training.

✐ **Medical and Health Services.** If you have an interest in health and wellness, consider a job in a hospital, nursing home, assisted-living facility, or physician's office.

These are just a few ideas showing how you can match your interests to a job. The best possible career for you is one in which you can do what you love doing. You can always change your mind, but begin now thinking about careers and jobs that interest you.

For You

OBJECTIVE

Describe your reason for wanting a job or for wanting to be accepted into an educational or training program.

_____

_____

Do you want a cash job or a career-related job?

_____

List three activities you enjoy and are interested in:

1. _____

2. _____

3. _____

For each of those activities, list a job you might be able to get now as a high school student. List jobs that match the activities listed above.

1. _____

2. _____

3. _____

Putting It Together

After you complete the worksheet called "Objective," you have what you need to finish the Job Resume Outline on pages 55-56. The only section remaining to be filled in is the objective. Take time to do that now.

Congratulations! You have written your first resume. You are ready to mail, e-mail, or post your resume. You can use what you have created as you search for jobs, internships, colleges, or other opportunities.

For You

RESUME ERRORS

Carefully proofread your resume. Then list any errors you found so they will serve as a reminder of things to watch for as you prepare future resumes. If you find an error on your paper resume, be sure to correct the error in your electronic resume file.

Errors noted in my first resume	Corrected
_____	_____
_____	_____
_____	_____
_____	_____
_____	_____
_____	_____

Job Leads

It's not pushy to tell people you are looking for a job or for a certain type of job. This is called networking, and this is the best way to find a job!

If you don't tell people you are looking for a job, they probably won't know, so tell people what you are looking for. Then they can keep their eyes open and tell you when they have heard of something that fits your skills, geographic area, and salary needs. Refer to "Networking" on page 15 for a review of networking.

On the following worksheet, list the names of three people you could consider to be part of your network. Name one teacher, one person who is a friend of one of your parents, and one other person (for example: a neighbor, former boss, coach, or church leader). Also list each person's telephone number and address.

For You

NETWORK

A teacher

Name, address, phone number:_____

_____

Friend of my parents'

Name, address, phone number:_____

_____

Another person

Name, address, phone number:_____

_____

Contact each of these people and anyone else you consider to be part of your network. Tell each of them that you're searching for a summer or part-time position. Tell them what kind of work you are interested in.

On page 10, under the heading "Finding Mentors," you did some research to locate someone who would be a suitable mentor for you. Be sure to tell that person that you are looking for a job. Tell them what kind of job you want.

Also talk to your parents about what you plan to do to find a job. Ask for and listen to their advice. They will have suggestions you might not think of.

When you contact your mentor or the people in your network, ask if they have any ideas where you could apply for work. Ask your parents, too. If any of these people say they don't have any suggestions right now, ask if you can call them back in a few days. Follow up to see if they think of any job leads. Most people will be willing to help you.

Handling Job Leads

When a job lead comes your way, get as much information as possible about the referred business or person. Here are two pointers on handling job leads:

- Take detailed notes about the potential employer. Write down the company name, telephone number, and address and any insight about the company that your contact may have. Research the company on the Internet for information about its mission, services, and customers. Read company press releases and job listings.

- Ask the person who gives you the lead how you should contact the employer—by phone, fax, mail, or some other way. Ask if you can use your contact's name when introducing yourself. It's great if you can mention someone's name as an introduction. If your contact suggests you call the employer, ask when would be a good time for calling. If your contact person suggests you approach the employer by fax or by mail, send your resume and a cover letter that mentions your contact's name at the beginning.

Calling About Job Leads

When you contact a person to whom you've been referred, you will most likely get his or her attention. You also will probably get at least a few minutes of time. This is because of the relationship the person has with your contact. When calling a referral, be clear, upbeat, confident, and friendly. Also be respectful of the person's time. Ask if he or she has a few minutes to talk. If the person is busy, ask when you can call back. Talk somewhat slowly. Remember that you are selling yourself!

You will benefit from writing a telephone script that you can follow when making your calls. Practice your telephone call on videotape or with a friend first. Here's a sample script:

You: Hi, my name is Kathy Weinstein. I was referred to you by my family's accountant, James Waters. I am a junior at Quincy High and will be majoring in business in college. I was wondering if I could send you my resume for consideration for any summer work you might have? I have good computer and administrative skills.

Potential employer: Sure, that would be fine. We usually hire one or two clerks for the summer. I'll think about it. Send your resume to me at 555 Main Street.

You: Thank you. Is it okay if I call you in a week to set up a meeting where we could discuss a summer position? I'm trying to line up something early.

Potential employer: Okay, call me again in a few days.

You: Thanks for your time. I'll put my resume in the mail today.

If the person is not interested in hiring summer help, you could ask if the company hires part-time workers during the school year. Even if the company is not hiring or is not interested, be polite. Thank the person for his or her time. Say that you might contact the company again in the future. No matter what the employer's response, send him or her a thank-you note. You never know when you may meet the person again.

Following a Lead

On Emily's resumes on pages 23 and 24, she lists an internship at a national park. Here's how she found out about the job.

Emily's mother visited a friend in Maui who had a friend who was the chief law enforcement officer at Haleakala National Park.

After getting the name and number from her mom's friend, Emily called the officer. She asked about volunteers and interns. The officer said that the park used interns and told Emily how to apply. Emily sent her resume. Within five months, she was accepted as an intern and went to live and work in Maui for three exciting months.

Print and Online Job Ads

The best jobs are usually not found in the want ads (also called classified ads). Most jobs are found through leads your friends and other people give you and through your own job search in your local area.

Still, you should read the classified ads online or in the newspaper. If you find a job you want to respond to, follow these steps:

- Print the advertisement on paper if it is online
- Underline the keywords and skills listed in the ad
- Edit your cover letter and resume to add a few of the keywords and skills
- Send the resume and letter by mail or e-mail, following the instructions in the job ad
- Keep a copy of the ad with the date you mailed your application

Here is an example of a classified ad with the key words underlined. If you were applying for this job, you would mention some of these words in the skills section of your resume. You would also use these words if you got an interview.

Circulation Clerk: Entry-level, part-time position. Duties include ensuring timely and accurate delivery of the newspaper, route scheduling, paper organization, and inventory management. Must be dependable and able to communicate with customers in person and by telephone. Send resume to jlthomas@baltimoresun.com.

Here's how to interpret the keywords in the ad:

- **Timely and accurate delivery.** The work probably starts early in the morning. You will help make sure newspapers are delivered on time. You might emphasize your record of completing school projects on time. You might mention that you often get up early to swim or attend club meetings before school.

- **Paper organization and inventory management.** You will be responsible for keeping organized records of the number of papers delivered and the money collected. You might emphasize your experience as sophomore class treasurer.

- **Able to communicate with customers.** You will be expected to answer customer inquiries and complaints about paper delivery and about payments due. You might emphasize your high school speech classes.

For You

KEYWORDS IN JOB ADS

Find four job ads in the newspaper or on the Internet. These should not be the same ads you chose in Chapter 1. Cut out or print out the four jobs and tape them in the space below.

List keywords used in the ads. List two of your skills or experiences you think would match each keyword.

Keywords in ad	My matching skills

Cold Calling

Cold calling in person takes a little bit of nerve, but it can pay off because you never know when a company will have an opening that suits you. Opportunities for cold calling are all around you. As you look around your town or neighborhood, do you see a company where you would like to work? Go into commercial buildings and read the directory of company names. Is there a company name that looks interesting? Look under the main headings in the yellow pages for companies of interest, too. You'll find many places to contact through cold calling.

Making Cold Calls in Person

Take this list with you if you need to be reminded of what to do. You can turn this into a script to make cold calls by phone.

- Go in the main door of the company.
- Talk to the receptionist.
- Ask for or pick up a company brochure.
- Ask if the company hires students for summer or part-time positions.
- Ask how you can apply for a position.
- Ask who you should see.
- Ask for an appointment.
- Ask if you can leave a resume for the hiring person.
- Ask when you should call back.

Result: The receptionist will be impressed with your initiative and will remember you. If the receptionist looks annoyed, ask questions anyway and be very nice. When he or she gives your resume to the supervisor, the receptionist may comment on how inquiring and determined you were.

Making Cold Calls Using E-Mail or the Internet

Using e-mail or the Internet to make cold calls is a little easier than making them in person. When you send an e-mail, you don't have to meet the other person face to face.

- Write to or e-mail the webmaster or a human resources person.
- Ask if the company is hiring high school students part-time or during summers. Also ask if the company offers internships.
- Someone from the company will write back or e-mail you to give you the information. If not, follow up with a telephone call.

✐ If the company does hire students, send your resume and cover letter to be entered into the company database.

Result: If you have skills that match the company's needs, you will probably be considered for a job.

Here's an example of an e-mail you might send. In the subject line, tell the name of the job or internship.

Dear Human Resources Officer:

I found your Web site and would like to know if you hire high school students part time during the school year or full time in the summer. I'd also like to know if you have any internship programs.

If you do, I would appreciate your letting me know. I would like to apply for these types of positions. I am planning to pursue a business degree after high school, and I would like to gain experience in a business such as the Marriott Corporation.

My skills are communication, computers (keyboard 45 wpm), and organization.

Thanks for your consideration. I look forward to your information.

Sincerely,

Scott Holland

Job Search Web Sites

Start with these search engines. Your library or school will have Internet access. Search under Employment Opportunities or use specific industry and job terms to find companies, keywords, and job listings:

www.planetedu.com/

www.coe.edu/careerservices/students/internships.html

www.altavista.digital.com

www.google.com

www.metacrawler.com

www.yahoo.com

www.lycos.com

www.monster.com

How do you find information about a certain job by using a search engine? If you have an interest in eldercare, for example, how would you find a summer job that relates to your interest? Follow these steps:

- Type in a keyword related to that career (for example, Assisted Living). Many related Web page addresses and facility names will appear.

- Click the pages that seem most relevant. Find facility names, locations, and contact information. Identify businesses in your area.

- Call or write (either a letter or an e-mail) the businesses in your area. Ask about summer and part-time positions.

- As you search the Web sites, look for the names and e-mail addresses of managers or personnel directors. If you can find only the webmaster's e-mail address, write and ask the webmaster for the manager's e-mail address.

Here is an example of an e-mail you might send in search of an internship. Again, in the subject line, identify the job you are interested in:

Dear Ms. Watkins:

I am interested in pursuing eldercare as a career and have visited your Web site. Your company's site is very impressive. I will be starting college in one year and am interested in gaining experience as a student intern. I believe that my excellent communication skills, past experience working with senior citizens, and computer abilities would be a good match for your company.

Please e-mail me about your application process. Please indicate the proper person to contact regarding an internship. I will then forward my resume for consideration. Thank you for your time.

Sincerely,

Jen Grine

If you receive a positive response, send your cover letter and resume by mail or e-mail. When sending a resume by e-mail, be sure to find out if the recipient can read attachments created in the word-processing program you use. Instead of an e-mail attachment, you may have to paste the resume inside the textbox of the e-mail.

For more information on job openings, internships, resume writing, job search strategies, volunteer positions, community service opportunities, government educational programs, colleges, and leadership possibilities, visit the following Web sites. (These sites were current at the time of publication.)

First try your local newspaper online, for example:

Baltimore Sun

www.baltimoresun.com

Find the Careers page

Washington Post

www.washingtonpost.com/wl/jobs/home

Find Washington Metropolitan Area Jobs

Search for job ads for part-time or summer listings that do not require a college degree. You might find that a local search for cash jobs will be the fastest. You know the companies in your neighborhood and can contact them directly instead of looking for listings online.

Government Jobs

The U.S. Government is the largest employer in America, with 1.8 million employees. This does not include the U.S. Postal Service, the U.S. Military, or contractors who work for the government. The government is hiring. You should consider government jobs or internships to begin your career and to gain valuable career experience. The job search is a little different than in private industry, but with effort, you can find an interesting and possibly good-paying position. You can find information at these sites:

- **www.nps.gov/youthprograms/**

    Provides information on youth programs in the National Park Service. If you enjoy the outdoors, you might look for a job as a parks worker or interpreter. Be sure you apply correctly and on time.

- **www.usajobs.opm.gov**

    Summer Jobs for Youth—Series 9999

    Click on FAQ at the top. Scroll down to Summer Jobs. Search in the job listings for "Summer 9999." The job listings will come up. You can use the telephone to search for job listings as well.

- **www.studentjobs.gov/index.htm**

    Student Jobs page for government jobs

- **www.americorps.gov/**

  Americorps Program

  Consider the Americorps when you are finished with high school if you would like to serve America in some way. You can gain great work experience and a stipend and begin your education or career. Also, your work may involve travel. For stories written by Americorps members, look at

  www.americorps.gov/joining/memberstories/member6.html

  www.americorps.gov/joining/pickprogram.html

- **www.nasajobs.nasa.gov/**

  NASA Student Jobs and Internships

  You can work for an important government agency as a student. Write your resume and apply for internships, cooperative programs, and stay-in-school programs.

- **www.cns.gov/serve.asp**

  Community service information

  Search for interesting jobs with nonprofit and service organizations.

- **www.firstgov.gov/Agencies/Federal/All_Agencies/index.shtml**

  If you are interested in finding internships and student job listings with a specific government agency, use the site above to find the Web site for the agency's main department. Go to the agency you are seeking and search under Student Internships or Student Jobs.

- **www.jobs.nih.gov/Programclosed.htm**

  This is the Web page for the National Institutes of Health Internships. This organization hires high school students into internship programs every year.

You may be wondering how you can qualify for a student position with a government agency. To be eligible for a student appointment, you must

- Be at least 16 years old

- Be enrolled or accepted for enrollment as a degree-seeking student (for example, a diploma or certificate)

- Be taking or be signed up to take at least a half-time academic, vocational, or technical course load

- Be enrolled in or accepted for enrollment in an accredited high school, technical, or vocational school, in a two- or four-year college or university, or in a graduate or professional school

Here are some suggestions:

- Contact the agency you wish to work for and apply directly to that agency. In cases where an agency has issued a vacancy announcement for a student position, the announcement will provide details on the position and the procedures to follow in applying for it.

- Search for government agencies in your area. Research them on the Internet. You can also call the Human Resources offices to see if the agencies are hiring high school students for stay-in-school programs, co-ops, or internships. You will be amazed at the good pay and benefits and at the great job skills you can develop in a government agency.

- Contact a military base in your local area, if there is one. The base probably has high school jobs, internships, co-op programs, community service opportunities, and stay-in-school programs. If you know someone who works at the base, ask that person for the human resources office telephone number and the name of someone to contact. Call that office to ask about high school jobs. Locate the base's Web site. Also, ask for the name, telephone number, and e-mail address of someone else you can contact.

If you get the phone number but no one answers the phone, leave a voicemail message like this:

My name is Lauren Scott. I live in Fishers, Indiana. I am a high school junior looking for an internship or part-time position. Please contact me to let me know whether you have positions or internships for students. Thanks for your time. My home number is (301) 555-5555.

Here are the Web pages for jobs for civilians (people who work for the military but do not join the military).

- **Navy and Marines:** www.donhr.navy.mil

  Human Resources e-mails for regional areas in the Navy: www.donhr.navy.mil/Jobs/ContactList.asp

  You can write to the e-mail addresses for your geographic region. Use the following as your subject line: "Student Job Inquiry, Please."

- **Army:** www.cpol.army.mil

- **Air Force:** http://www.afpc.randolph.af.mil/

Internships

The following Web sites give information on internships. You can use the internship experience for community service or career experience.

www.internjobs.com

www.campusinternships.com

www.careerbuilder.com

campus.monster.com/

www.petersons.com/

www.washingtonpost.com/wl/jobs/home

www.coolworks.com/

www.careerplanit.com/world/internship.cfm

www.acm.org/student/internships.html

www.internships.wctfeet.com/home.asp

www.idealist.org/

www.4work.com/

For You

WEB SITE REVIEW

Visit three of the Web sites listed in this chapter. Write two sentences about what you learned at each site.

Web site: _____

What I learned: _____

_____

Web site: _____

What I learned: _____

_____

Web site: _____

What I learned: _____

_____

Interview Tips

So it's your big day. You have an appointment for an interview. Keep the following pointers in mind:

- Wear nice clothes (no jeans) that fit the company's image. You should be dressed similar to the way everyone else at the company dresses. If you don't know how to dress, visit the company before the day of your interview. Look at employees' clothes. For example, if you're a male interviewing at a corporate office, you should wear a sports coat, tie, and slacks. If you're a female, wear a nice dress, stockings, and shoes with toes. Wear almost no jewelry, reasonable makeup, and a conservative hairstyle. If you're applying to a clothing retailer, wear good pants and a sweater that looks like they could have been bought at that store.

- Wear very little cologne or perfume, or none at all. Some people are allergic to colognes.

- Be confident. If an employer hires you, he or she is getting a good employee, right? You'll help the company take care of customers, organize its store, or handle other important activities. Think positively.

- Show up a few minutes early. Don't get stressed out rushing, running, going through yellow lights, getting a speeding ticket, getting lost, and wrecking your outfit. Start early and stay calm.

- Don't be afraid to make yourself sound great. It's okay to say you're good at a few things. You are selling yourself, and you want to get hired. Tell the interviewer why the company should hire you—because you can speak very comfortably with the public, because you're dependable and responsible, and because you would like to get experience doing this work. An employer likes a person who knows his or her strengths. Memorize your list of strengths. Think of stories that will demonstrate your ability to do a good job.

- Call at least a day ahead if you need to reschedule an interview. It's okay to reschedule if something unavoidable comes up. Companies are usually accommodating if you give notice.

- Look the interviewer in the eye. Don't look down.

- Smile when you can.

- Breathe naturally and try to relax.

- Keep your resume in an attractive folder, not crumpled in your pocket or purse. Go to an office supply store and buy a folder or notebook to hold your resume and reference sheet.

- Do not take backpacks, athletic bags, water bottles, books, or huge pocketbooks to an interview. Take only a small folder or notebook. If you are a girl, you can also take a small purse.

- Do not give your prospective employer an incomplete application or an out-of-date resume. Double-check your application. Update your resume before the interview so the interviewer does not have to ask questions that waste time. An interviewer will not appreciate your lack of consideration.

- Bring a pen and notepad. Take a few notes in the interview. You will need these notes for writing your thank-you letter. Be sure to get the correct spelling and pronunciation of the interviewer's name and his or her title. Get a business card if you can.

- Ask questions. Research the company before going to the interview. Find out how long the company has been in business, how many employees it has, how many states it operates in, and what its products or services are. Ask questions about the company's growth and goals. Employers appreciate the opportunity to answer questions instead of always asking questions. They will like your curiosity and interest.

- Watch your posture and don't put your hands in your pockets. Try to look sharp by standing up straight and looking friendly.

- Be yourself. It's okay to be young. The employer knows that you're in high school and that you want experience and the chance to earn some money.

- Maintain eye contact with the interviewer when you are asked questions and are giving answers. This is very important.

- Do not speak negatively of yourself or a former employer. Skip all the bad history. For example, don't say you left your last job because the hours were too early and you're not a morning person. Do not tell the interviewer that you did not get along with your last supervisor. Talk only about the good things. Interviewers are not impressed with anything negative. Stick with the positives about you and your experiences.

- Do not bring food, drinks, or gum to an interview. This is messy and absolutely not professional.

- Be polite. It's most important that you have good manners and say thank you after the interview.

- Be prepared. Take extra resumes and bring your reference list.

For You

INTERVIEW PREPARATION

List highlights of your education, experience, skills, and background to discuss in an interview. Refer to your resume for ideas.

_____

_____

_____

_____

Write your job-related strengths here and memorize this list.

_____

_____

_____

_____

Write your answer to the interview question, "Tell me a little about yourself."

_____

_____

_____

_____

Write your answer to the interview question, "What can you offer my company?"

_____

_____

_____

_____

The resumes of these new high school graduates will look a lot different in just a few years.

WHAT'S NEXT?

Congratulations! You have completed this workbook and your resume. The next step is to use your resume and apply for jobs consistently. If you do, you will be an accomplished job seeker even though you are just in high school. The job seeking skills you learn now will be effective throughout your career. Remember to be persistent, committed, positive, and upbeat. Think about your next job while you are in a current job.

Best wishes to you as you begin your career and job search. If you have a job search success story to share, please e-mail me at kathryn@resume-place.com.

Index